MILESTONES

The First 75 Years of ABWE's Journey

ASSOCIATION OF BAPTISTS FOR WORLD EVANGELISM

P.O. Box 8585 • Harrisburg, PA 17105-8585 • 717.774.7000 • abwe@abwe.org

ABWE CANADA

160 Adelaide St. South, Suite 205 • London, Ontario N5Z 3L1 • 519.690.1009 • office@abwecanada.org

ABWE PUBLISHING

MILESTONES: The First 75 Years of ABWE's Journey
Copyright © 2002 by ABWE Publishing

Library of Congress Cataloguing-in-Publications Data (application pending)
MILESTONES: The First 75 Years of ABWE's Journey
Missions, Non-fiction
International Standard Book Number: 1-888796-28-6

Printed in the United States of America

MILESTONES

Since ancient times, milestones have marked the location and distance for travelers on a journey. Thousands of milestones still exist today along highways built by Roman legions as they marched to conquer and secure the empire.

 In the year 2002 AD, the Association of Baptists for World Evangelism celebrates a seventy-five-year journey from our humble beginning in the Philippines to the many nations on every continent where we serve today. Now we pause to look back at the markers that remind us where we have been and where we are headed.

We won't have time to pause by every single milestone. Rather, we intend to stop by several significant and symbolic ones. Some milestones will call to memory key turning points. Others will recall periods of exhausting effort, and some will be places where we ran with glee. Some milestones mark the graves of fallen comrades and call us to the holy hush of sacred ground. All will remind us that One who paved the way called us to make the journey.

We may consider stretches of road worn smooth by many feet, reminding us that none of us walk this journey alone. We are surrounded by those who encouraged, supported, and loved us.

This journey is the path of blistered feet, beautiful as they ran with the gospel to the ends of the earth. We desire to learn from the milestones of the past, in order to meet the challenge of the future, for the journey has just begun.

Michael G. Loftis

"I beheld, and, lo, a great multitude, which no man could number, of all nations, and kindreds, and people, and tongues, stood before the throne."

—Revelation 7:9

CONTENTS

I once heard a successful leader say, "We Baptists have done a good job making history, but a very poor one writing it." Our exploits of dedication often have centered on doing, while the discipline of writing our history has languished.

The writers and researchers of this volume attempt to capture the glorious events of the Association of Baptists for World Evangelism over the past 75 years. They could not possibly report every detail, but rather have provided a literary mirror that most accurately reflects the major events of this mission organization.

The writings and photographs wonderfully testify God's birthing of ABWE and the marvelous way He has sustained it since 1927. Each page is stained with the sacrifice and commitment of modern-day soldiers of Jesus Christ. We read of the men and women who valiantly served on the front lines year after year. They were courageous in battle, strong in biblical convictions, steadfast in the faith, evangelists in their hearts, dedicated to church planting, and obedient to their call.

And they would testify in one voice, "Without God, our story would not be possible. The ink of God's faithfulness has written every page." Therefore, God alone must be glorified. His Son must be exalted. We must again acknowledge His mighty acts. Our entire ABWE family humbly accepts the joyful privilege of being His instruments of preaching and teaching the precious gospel of the Lord Jesus Christ throughout the world. Our hearts overflow with praise and thanksgiving.

So I invite you, "Come and see the works of God who is awesome in deeds toward the sons of men" (Psalm 66:50).

Great things He hath done . . .
over and over again,

Wendell W. Kempton

"Give unto the LORD the glory due unto his name; worship the LORD in the beauty of holiness."

—Psalm 29:2

Raphael Thomas was an ordained minister and medical doctor with degrees from Andover-Newton Theological Seminary and the Harvard Medical College. He administered the hospital in Iloilo, Philippines, where he had served for 25 years.

Some of Dr. Thomas' missionary colleagues criticized him for spending too much time in evangelism and not enough time in the hospital. His home board ordered him to stop his itinerant evangelism and devote himself to the hospital. Since evangelism was his first priority, Raphael Thomas resigned in 1927 from the American Baptist Foreign Mission Society. This led to the founding of ABEO.

Norma Thomas, daughter of Norman Waterbury and Lucy Waterbury Peabody, graduated from Vassar College, won the Sargent Prize at Harvard College, and authored the *Jack and Janet* series of junior mission books.

> "*Every doctor in a mission hospital should be an evangelist.*"
>
> —Dr. R. C. Thomas

Raphael and Norma Thomas with son Burgess

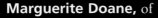

Marguerite Doane, of Watch Hill, Rhode Island, was the daughter of well-known musician and inventor William Howard Doane. At Mr. Doane's death, he left his estate to his daughters, who established the Houses of Fellowship—among other philanthropies—for missionaries on furlough.

In August 1927, Mrs. Doane invited a dozen concerned friends, including the Peabodys and Thomases, to her home. After lengthy discussion and prayer, they decided to establish a new mission. Mrs. Peabody was chairwoman of the sponsoring committee; Frederic Crawford, a lawyer from Boston, became secretary and agreed to draw up the papers of incorporation; Hilda Olson served as the first treasurer, and Mrs. Doane agreed to serve as chairman of the finance committee.

The mission's name was carefully selected. The Association of Baptists for Evangelism in the Orient was to be an **association** rather than a convention, to indicate a voluntary banding together of like-minded Baptist missionaries with the primary task of **evangelism.** Their field of endeavor would be enlarged from the Philippines to cover the **Orient.**

January 3, 2005

Dear Pastor,

Thank you so much for taking the time to respond to our questionnaire.

Your answers will be advantageous to us as we look to the future and try and determine how we can best serve your ministry. Our desire is to be servants of the local church for the sake of the gospel and world evangelism.

In appreciation for your response I am sending you a copy of our 75th Anniversary pictorial history coffee table book titled, "Milestones." I hope this is a blessing to you.

The vision of our publishing ministry is to let churches and individuals know what God is doing around the world. We want to provide missions minded churches with resources no longer provided in the broader Christian market. I am also including a copy of our ABWE Publishing resource catalogue so you may be aware of materials that may be of help in your ministry. [I.E.: curriculum, book store supplies, library materials, adult Bible study materials, biographies, sermon illustrations, children's materials, missionary skits, drama, music, etc.]

May the Lord bless your ministry for the glory of God and the advance of the gospel.

Yours in the Harvest,

E.C. Haskell
Executive Administrator of Mission Relations
II Corinthians 4:7

American Baptist
Mission Hospital, Jaro, Iloilo

The Thomases' co-workers who shared their convictions and also resigned from the American Baptist Foreign Mission Society:

- Helen Hinkley, daughter of a Baptist pastor, served with the Thomases in Iloilo.
- Ellen Martien, dean of women at Stetson College in Florida before becoming a missionary in the Philippines, served in many teaching positions at the Doane Baptist Bible Institute.
- Bessie Traber, graduate of Vassar College and the Biblical Seminary of New York, taught college students before serving in the Philippines at her own expense. After years of missionary service, she founded the Bible Club Movement (now BCM International).
- Alice Drake, graduate of Moody Bible Institute, was traveling around the world visiting missionaries when she clearly sensed God calling her back to the Philippines. She waited in Cairo, Egypt, for her parents' consent before returning to the work in Iloilo.

Esther Yerger

From left: Miss Esther Yerger, Miss Bessie Traber, Mrs. George W. (Marguerite) Doane,
Mrs. Lucy Peabody, Miss Alice Hudson, Miss Ruth Woodworth, Miss Alice Drake

"A work of faith, though small, unknown, unpublished, yet may be God's foothold for things of which you cannot dream and if told now, you would not possibly believe."

—G. Campbell Morgan

PEABODY

COMMONS

P R E S I

KEMPTON

LOFTIS

D   E   N   T   S

LUCY WATERBURY PEABODY
(1927–1935)

"Said a stylish young woman, 'Missionaries look so bedraggled!' Bless them! So do soldiers just home from war, and instead of smiling at their scars, worn-out uniforms, and limping gait, we offer cheers of homage and sympathy to those who have borne the cross in loyalty and patriotism."

—Lucy Peabody,
A Wider World for Women

Lucy served as a missionary among Telugu-speakers in India, until her husband died in 1886, leaving her with two small children. She returned to the United States and became a teacher, writer, editor, and public speaker. Rising to prominence in the Northern Baptist Conven-

tion, she served as secretary of the Women's American Baptist Foreign Mission Society for 18 years.

In 1904, Lucy married Henry Wayland Peabody. For the rest of her life, she lived in Beverly, Massachusetts, helping many worthy causes.

At Marguerite Doane's

summer cottage in Watch Hill, Rhode Island, in 1927, Mrs. Peabody helped form an independent Baptist mission agency known as the Association of Baptists for Evangelism in the Orient. Lucy Peabody was elected as the first president and served in that capacity for more than seven years.

HAROLD TABER COMMONS
(1935–1971)

"Sometimes we make plans and they do not work . . . We are not opposed to making plans. In fact the man who never made a plan never made anything. Sometimes, however, it seems that our most successful efforts have resulted through circumstances created by others and laid upon our doorstep."

—Harold Commons,
Heritage and Harvest

Harold's relationship with ABWE began in 1931 through his friendship with board member David Otis Fuller. Since the roster was full, Harold could not join the board, but Mrs. Peabody considered Harold Commons a "promising young man," and he served as secretary to the board.

Harold Commons was elected a member of the ABWE board in 1933, then vice president in 1934. At the April 1935 board meeting, Lucy Peabody resigned as president and Harold Commons was named her successor. He guided ABWE through many difficult years, including World War II.

When Harold Commons assumed the office of president, ABWE had 18 missionaries working only in the Philippines. When he retired, 350 missionaries served in 11 countries.

WENDELL WALKER KEMPTON

(1971–2001)

"This whole business is a corporate giant step of faith every day, and yet it is a single step of faith by each one involved."

—Wendell Kempton

As ABWE's presidential search committee looked for a successor to Harold Commons, they considered Wendell Kempton's evangelistic fervor, passion for preparing young adults to serve the Lord, and leadership skills. Wendell Kempton became ABWE's third president in June 1971.

During the next 30 years the number of ABWE missionaries grew from 350 to over 1,000 serving in more than 60 countries. Under Wendell's leadership, ABWE moved from Philadelphia to Cherry Hill and then to Harrisburg.

Wendell's tenure at ABWE included frequent travels; he encouraged missionaries and nationals, represented ABWE in churches and schools, and developed a network of people interested in missions.

He became president-emeritus in March 2001.

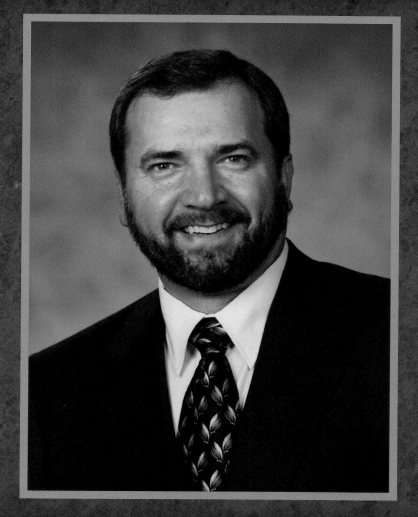

MICHAEL GRAYSON LOFTIS
(2001–)

"You and I have been chosen by God to reach ONE generation— OURS."

—**Michael G. Loftis**

Michael grew up as the son of missionary church planters in Jamaica before joining the faculty of Tennessee Temple University and serving with his wife, Jo Beth, in four Baptist churches.

In 1986, Wendell Kempton invited Michael and Jo Beth to join him on an evangelistic trip to Romania. Several weeks later, the Loftises committed to join ABWE, developing leadership training behind the Iron Curtain. No one anticipated the collapse of communism in the 1990s, which made countries more accessible to the gospel.

For 12 years Michael served as executive administrator for Central and Eastern Europe, building a team of over 70 career missionaries serving in nine countries.

Following a two-year search process, the ABWE board extended a unanimous call to Michael Loftis

"Declare His marvelous works among all nations."

SHINE AS LIGHTS IN THE WORLD
1927 2002

WORLD
EVANGELISM

WORLD

EVANGELISM

REGIONAL CHURCH-PLANTING AND THEOLOGICAL EDUCATION

(Countries listed in chronological order of opening)

THE FAR EAST

EXECUTIVE ADMINISTRATORS FOR THE FAR EAST

Russell E. Ebersole, Jr.

After serving from 1953 as a church planter and administrator in the Philippines, Russ Ebersole's missionary career was interrupted when his wife and missionary partner, Gene (DeVries), died in 1964. Russ then served in the ABWE office. In 1969, Russ married Nancy Goehring, whose husband Harry had died in East Pakistan. Along with Nancy, Russ returned to the Philippines until 1977 when he was appointed executive administrator for the Far East. He served in that capacity until 1995.

William T. Commons

Bill and Sharon Commons served as missionaries in Hong Kong for 15 years, followed by 15 years leading ABWE's enlistment department. In 1995, Bill received the baton of Far East administration from Russ Ebersole, serving in this capacity until 2002.

Kent A. Craig

Kent and Kelly Craig served three terms in the Philippines in church planting and administrative ministries. In 2002, he succeeded Bill Commons as executive administrator for the Far East.

PHILIPPINES

It all began 75 years ago in Iloilo City, Philippines, when Dr. Raphael Thomas chose the priority of preaching the gospel over the security of a career in medical social work. From the initial group of four, Association of Baptists for Evangelism in the Orient (ABEO, now ABWE) spread throughout the Philippine archipelago and the world.

Evangelism, church planting, and the training of national leaders have been hallmarks of ABWE since its inception.

The original Doane Baptist Seminary building in Iloilo, Philippines, was built in 1927.

Mona Kemery (left) and Ruth Woodworth (front) with two Solidarios sisters in Iloilo

Monument commemorating MacArthur's landing on Leyte

In 1929, Dr. Thomas established the First Baptist Church and the Baptist Bible Seminary and Institute in Manila. The island of Palawan became part of ABEO's responsibility in 1930 as *The Gospel Ship*, under Captain Ellis Skolfield, carried the gospel to many unreached areas.

Despite their grueling experience in prison camp, Ed and Marian Bomm stayed after World War II to work among the American GI's.

MANILA·EVANGELISTIC·INSTITUTE

Russ Ebersole and other
missionaries planted churches
in the provincial villages.

"An army of fearless and trained Filipino men and women went anywhere, with or without pay, preaching the unsearchable riches of Christ."

—Marian Bomm

Filipino pastors and ABWE missionaries have planted more than 1,500 churches. In the 1960s, the Philippine Association of Baptists for World Evangelism (PABWE) was formed. PABWE continues to send missionaries to other Asian countries.

Kay Friederichsen's cartoons boosted morale in the internment camp. "Joe Internee" hoped Uncle Sam would soon come to his graduation.

PROJECT HOPE

Project HOPE (Helping Open People's Eyes) was developed in 1990 to allow North American pastors to team up with Filipino counterparts in conducting evangelistic campaigns in the Philippines. During the first two-week venture, 53 men from North America preached in churches, homes, schools, jails, and many other settings.

Project HOPE II took place in 1998. Rev. Dan Gelatt, ABWE's international administrator for evangelism and church growth, has been key in organizing these pastors' outreaches.

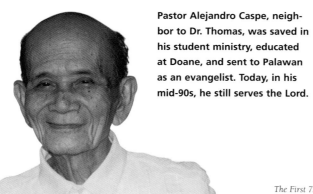

Pastor Alejandro Caspe, neighbor to Dr. Thomas, was saved in his student ministry, educated at Doane, and sent to Palawan as an evangelist. Today, in his mid-90s, he still serves the Lord.

HONG KONG

Gathering of "old Hong Kong hands" at the 50th Anniversary celebration, October 2001

When the communists overran China, Victor and Margaret Barnett escaped to Hong Kong, where they worked from 1951 to 1955. Many Chinese believers also fled to Hong Kong, forming the foundation of Evangel Baptist Church.

The China Baptist Theological College (formerly Hong Kong Baptist Bible Institute) was started in 1966. The school, under its Chinese president, Dr. Teddy Cheng, is now governed by its own independent board and has a predominately local administrative staff and faculty.

The Hong Kong Fellowship of Churches sponsors a ministry among Filipina workers in Hong Kong, and missionaries in Sudan, Melanesia, northern Thailand, and other Asian countries.

Professors Harry Ambacher and Norm Barnard at the China Baptist Theological College

Jay Morgan teaches young people at camp on a sultry summer's day.

Bob Henry baptizes a new believer from the church in Happy Valley.

JAPAN

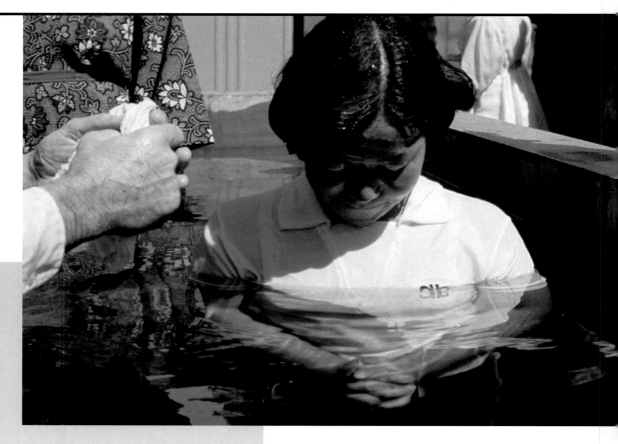

Baptism publicly identifies a person as a Christian and often results in persecution.

Camp continues to be an important part of evangelism. Unlike the missionaries, the children never tire of long days at camp.

A survey conducted in 1952 guided ABWE to center its work in the southern island of Kyushu, particularly Kagoshima Prefecture, when the first missionaries arrived in 1953.

In the 1960s, the Chandlers left the Kagoshima area to plant churches in the Kobe area of central Japan. Similarly, the Gerald Winters family moved to Fukuoka City in the northern part of Kyushu Island.

First summer camp in South Kyushu: Jay Morgan and Vern Chandler are on the left in the back; Paul Shook is on the right.

Shortly after Paul and Vada Shook were appointed to Japan in the fall of 1952, they learned that one of their twin sons was deaf. This resulted in a specialized ministry with the deaf in Kagoshima City and in other parts of Japan.

Today ABWE still works in the heavily populated suburb of Kobe, and in the beautiful mountains of South Kyushu. Ministries center on leadership training and church planting through teaching conversational English, cooking classes, sports, Camp Shalom, and outreach to the hearing impaired.

Miyodani Baptist Church was started under the ministry of the Chandlers in the Kobe area.

Sue Hahn, church-planting assistant, ministers to a young woman.

Vern Chandler, on the sax, and his son Mark, on the trumpet, provide special music in a tent meeting.

Winnifred Barnard and daughter Laura Anne travel to the hill tracts.

The Victor Barnard and Paul Miller families first trekked into the Chittagong Hill Tracts in 1957. They purchased the Hebron property, where missionaries operated a clinic and began translating the gospel into tribal languages. Thus a foundation was laid for fruitful work among the tribal people, a fact testified today by the presence of more than 120 "Jesus houses" (churches) that dot the hills.

The port city of Chittagong has played a major role in ABWE's work in Bangladesh. In 1962, Gene Gurganus started the Bible Correspondence School (BCS), which introduced the gospel to thousands in the following years. Today, the son of one of the first converts among the tribal people heads BCS. Bible translation and the Literature Division also are located in Chittagong.

Dr. Viggo and Joan Olsen arrived in 1962 to establish medical evangelism at Memorial Christian Hospital.

Many other effective ministries include Deshari Camp, AWANA, the Baptist Bible College of Bangladesh, and William Carey Academy.

Jay Walsh and Ancherai, "the Apostle Paul of the tribes"

Gene Gurganus speaks at a Bible Correspondence School rally.

"I just love this school . . . I never knew God loved me so much."
—William Carey Academy student

Stretching at William Carey Academy

**The Body of Christ
in Bangladesh**

**"You can't harvest a crop
unless you plant the
seeds. Often the seed
is Christian literature."**
—Jeannie Lockerbie

PAPUA NEW GUINEA

David and Joan Gardner were assigned to this new field in 1967, and with the arrival of additional missionaries, a church was started and Goroka Baptist Bible College was established.

ABWE missionaries and national workers have planted fifty churches in the eastern highland provinces and in two other towns. Aviation ministries make it possible to penetrate remote areas.

Headhunting and cannibalism characterized the tribes in Papua New Guinea for many years.

Missionary kids often charm their way into the hearts of the villagers.

"Missions is climbing over walls, over mountains, advancing into enemy territory."

—Ed Bomm

Dr. Don Jennings and David Gardner lead the procession of faculty and graduates of Goroka Baptist Bible College.

Training the women in literacy and Bible is vital to church planting.

Rich Ernst talks with John, a Christian worker.

Grace Baptist Church in Port Moresby, the nation's capital, was established along with a flourishing student ministry at the University of Papua New Guinea.

AUSTRALIA

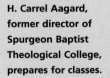

H. Carrel Aagard, former director of Spurgeon Baptist Theological College, prepares for classes.

Veteran missionaries

Larry and Jacqui Armstrong opened the field in 1971. The greater Sydney area was targeted for a church-planting thrust.

A team that included missionaries who transferred from Chile and the Philippines, along with new recruits, planted churches and launched Spurgeon Baptist Theological College to train pastors and church leaders.

ABWE missionaries teach Bible in public schools, hold marriage and parenting sem-

"A" Team members Dave Toro (center) and John Baker (right) with guests

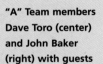

John Baker with a boys' Scripture class

Another method of evangelism—sports as a drawing card

inars, and host neighborhood teas, children's clubs, and other events. Through their efforts, six churches have been started. Church-planting teams continue to use innovative ways to reach a population who state they "don't have time for religion."

The Larry Armstrong family, 1970

Connie Duty and famous furry friend

THAILAND & CAMBODIA

PABWE missionaries followed the Philippine model in starting churches through student ministries.

ศูนย์นักศึกษา
แบ๊พติสบางมด
BANGMOD BAPTIST STUDENT CENTER
สนับสนุนโดยองค์การแบ๊พติสฟิลิปปินส์ (P.A.B.W.E.) และกลุ่มแบ๊พติสร่มพระคุณ

Don and Gail Craft learned two languages to work among Thai tribes.

The traditional Thai greeting: "Sawasdee"

ABWE's interest in Thailand dates from 1963 when churches in the Philippines sent their first missionary there under the newly formed Philippine Association of Baptists for World Evangelism (PABWE).

At the invitation of PABWE, Don and Gail Craft, Thai-speaking missionaries, joined ABWE in 1996. Since 1999, they have worked under the leadership of PABWE missionaries Art and Phoebe Inion.

Art Inion, here (left) with a Thai believer, overcame painful shyness to serve with PABWE for over 30 years.

In 1997, God led veteran
missionaries Jim and Shirlie
Moore to pioneer the work
in Phnom Penh. Other
missionaries joined them.
Through Bible studies and
personal contacts, groups of
new believers are forming.
Reaching out to the thou-
sands of street children
has won many families to
Christ. The first church
plant, New Heart Baptist
Church, has about 60
baptized believers.

Street children
study God's Word
at the ministry
center.

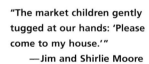

**"The market children gently
tugged at our hands: 'Please
come to my house.'"**
        —Jim and Shirlie Moore

**Rob Cady introduces
Cambodians to basic
Bible knowledge.**

MONGOLIA

Chris and Nicole Pilet arrived in the capital city of Ulaan Baatar in 2000. Since then, additional personnel have joined them to help pioneer ABWE's work in Mongolia.

Chris Pilet was first chair in our outreach to Mongolia.

(Right) The land of Genghis Khan

Ann DenUyl and a Mongolian man in front of a *ger*—a traditional Mongolian home

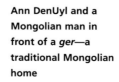

*"We are not called to be comfortable,
but to push back the darkness."*
—Wendell Kempton

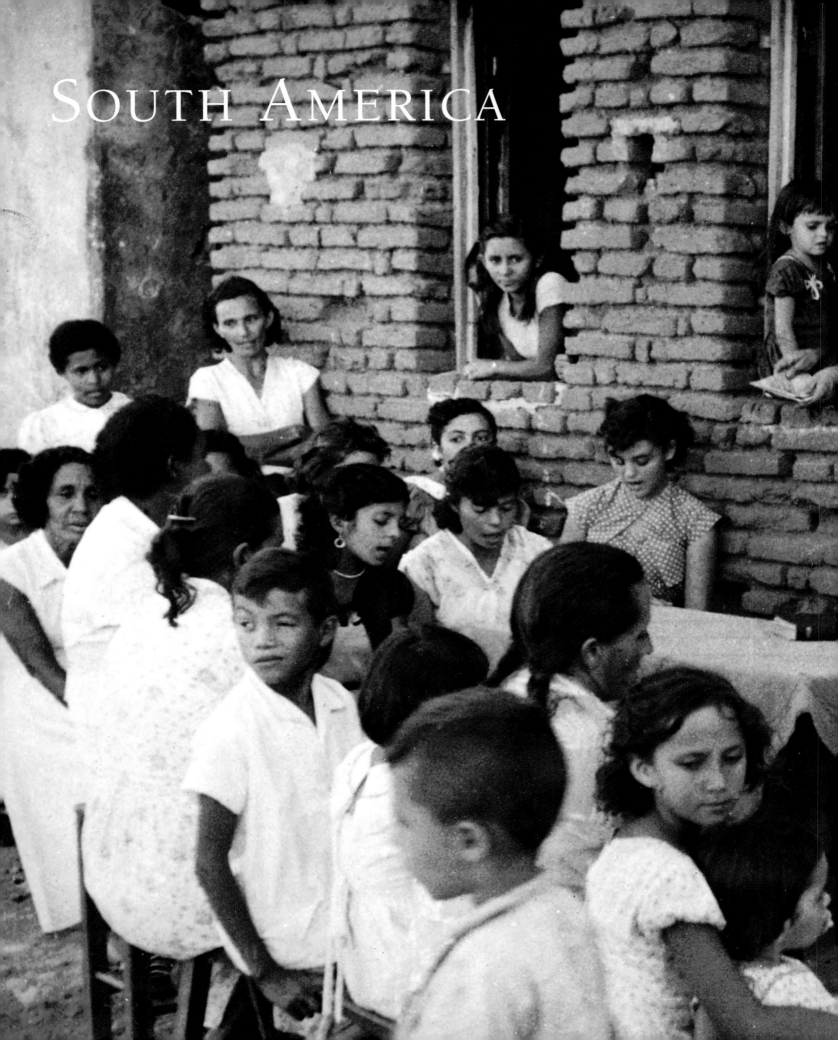

EXECUTIVE ADMINISTRATORS FOR SOUTH AMERICA

William J. Hopewell, Jr.
Bill and Ruth Hopewell joined ABWE in 1947, serving in the Philippines and Chile and then teaching for 11 years at Baptist Bible Seminary in Johnson City, New York. In 1967, Bill was called to serve as ABWE's deputation secretary. From 1977 to 1983, Bill was in charge of the South America, Europe, and Africa fields.

Arthur M. Cavey
Art and Joyce Cavey served in Brazil from 1951 to 1982. Art followed Bill Hopewell as executive administrator for South America from 1983 until he retired in 1993.

David B. Southwell
Dave and Evelyn Southwell served as missionaries in Brazil and then Portugal for 18 years. In 1993, Dave assumed the position of executive administrator for South America.

Bill and Elva Scherer were appointed in 1938 to return to the Amazon River region where they worked independently since 1931. With missionaries in South America, ABEO changed its name to the Association of Baptists for World Evangelism (ABWE).

With a growing missionary force, new churches were started in Iquitos and in remote river towns, accessed by boats and later by floatplanes. ABWE founded the Iquitos Baptist Bible Institute in 1948. Theological Education by Extension (TEE) and short-term Bible institutes train national leaders for service in their local churches.

After several years of concentrating on the jungle area, Don and Vivian Bond and other missionaries transferred to plant churches in coastal Peru cities, including Nazca, Arequipa, and Ica. A seminary, two campgrounds, an English immersion elementary school, and crisis pregnancy center in Lima enhance the church-planting efforts in coastal Peru.

Historic La Casona building, now home to New Life Baptist Church in Arequipa

The launch which carried Chuck Porter and TEE to river villages

> *"There is something about God that is so universally praiseworthy and so profoundly beautiful and so comprehensively worthy and so deeply satisfying, that God will find passionate admirers in every diverse people group in the world."*
> —John Piper, *Let the Nations be Glad*

Bill and Elva Scherer

**Jim Bowers
(far left) trains
national leaders.**

BRAZIL

Carleton and Mary

Adelaide Matthews opened northeast Brazil for ABWE in 1944. A recreational facility on the shores of Lake Bom Fim became a camp where the Berean Baptist Bible Institute and Seminary was started. The school later moved into the city of Natal. Scores of churches—many of them started by Brazilians—now cover the state.

Ticuna-built meeting hall

Four sisters, all saved under the Matthewses' ministry over 50 years ago, still sing for the Lord.

Carleton Matthews

Pastor Jaco and Art Cavey greet the graduates at São Paulo Seminary.

The Hare family in 1962; today three of the four daughters are ABWE missionaries.

ABWE missionaries then moved into Amazonas, Brazil, in 1950. They established a church and began using a launch to evangelize villages. In 1951, work began 100 miles downriver with unevangelized people, including Ticuna Indians.

When Don and Helen Hare moved from the northeast to care for their daughter's poor health in 1951, Brazilians were pouring into São Paulo by the thousands to take advantage of jobs in industry. Art and Joyce Cavey and many others joined the Hares in holding evangelistic tent meetings. Later portable tabernacles were erected on open lots to begin new churches.

In 1957, Don Hare and colleagues opened the Baptist Bible Institute and Seminary. It now has a Brazilian director, many Brazilian teachers, and offers master's-level courses.

In the early 1950s, ABWE missionaries established a working relationship with Brazilian pastors in Recife. Camp Paradise opened in 1965. Today a joint Brazilian/missionary board administers the camp.

In November 1998, Koinonia Baptist Church sent its first local missionaries to plant a church in the interior.

Lynell Smith
teaches a
children's
club in Belo
Horizonte.

Four children
from the Belo
Horizonte
boys' home

Willard and Grace Stull arrived in Belo Horizonte in 1966. They started children's Bible clubs, which served as the basis for Faith Baptist Church. In the following years, a camp, a sports center, and the Baptist Boys' Home were started in conjunction with Brazilian pastors and Christian workers.

ABWE opened its work in Bahia as missionaries transferred from other parts of Brazil. As the Bucks and other missionaries contacted occupants in local housing developments, Brazilians came to Christ and began to form churches. A seminary was recently opened to train local church leaders.

Brazilian pastors in Pôrto Alegre issued an invitation for ABWE to partner with them. In 1995, Dan and Diana Richner joined a Brazilian missionary to start a church in Novo Hamburgo.

After 14 years in northeast Brazil, Tom and Nancy Farlow made contacts for a new church plant in Campo Grande. Bible studies and contacts develop the nucleus from which a congregation will be formed.

The first missionaries arrived in Bauru, São Paulo state, in 2000 to open ABWE's newest work in Brazil.

Faith Baptist Church in Novo Hamburgo was the first ABWE church plant in South Brazil.

Tom Farlow surveys for a new church-planting thrust.

COLOMBIA

El Mensajero carried the Flodens to villages where there was not even a Bible.

Orville and Helen Floden were the first evangelical missionaries to stay in Leticia.

"Construction evangelism": Victor Ussa was saved during the building of the camp facilities.

Orville and Helen Floden arrived in 1944, working in Leticia for 30 years. They established a church, pastored since 1975 by a Colombian who studied at the Bible institute in Iquitos, Peru. The Flodens also carried on a ministry to towns and villages along the Amazon River in Colombia and Peru.

The first ABWE missionaries to work in Bogotá, the capital of Colombia, were Terry and Jean Armstrong, who transferred from Lima, Peru, in 1975. Two other families joined them in 1978, the same year an MK school started. Several churches were established in the city, as well as a Bible institute in 1980. In 1997, rural property was purchased to develop as a camp and conference center.

> *"What Colombia needs is not Christ on their lips, but Christ in their hearts. If religion would save a soul there would be no need of missionaries here . . ."*
>
> —Robert C. Savage

La Serena Baptist Church was the first church planted in Bogotá.

Geoff Williams and Bob Trout talk with the pastor in La Molina.

Camp under construction

Despite the challenges posed by terrorists, bombings, and guerrilla activities, ABWE has helped to establish 17 churches in and around Bogotá, and has graduated more than 250 students from the Bible institute.

A group of independent Baptist churches in Chile asked ABWE to provide Bible training for their pastors. In 1953, the Craymer and Olsen families transferred from Peru to Chile where Bill and Ruth Hopewell joined them.

Muriel Waite teaches students at Santiago Christian Academy

"How can ABWE and its missionaries adequately do the job of reaching the 'Long Land of Plenty' with the mercy of God? The Lord's people at home must bombard the throne of grace for Chile and the work to be done."

—*Message,* February 1953

Bud Craymer returns from the survey of Chile in 1952.

Additional missionaries arrived on the field and, in 1968, Larry and Bev Smith started Santiago Christian Academy, an MK school, and moved the Bible institute to downtown Santiago. Mission trips that were part of the institute curriculum gave birth to a national missionary movement operated entirely by Chileans.

While most of the early efforts in Chile concentrated in Santiago, missionaries later spread to other areas. ABWE currently cooperates with 25 local churches.

The Dyksterhouses and Hopewells

PARAGUAY

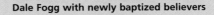
Dale Fogg with newly baptized believers

In 1974, Bob and Lynne Trout transferred from Lima, Peru. Joined by others, including the Collier and Fields families, they planted churches in the capital city of Asunción and the suburbs of San Pablo and Lambaré.

Reaching interior cities soon became the focus of ministry, and congregations sprouted up throughout the country.

Camp dining hall

The Source of Light

Bible correspondence school, a 70-acre camp, and an evening Bible institute program support church-planting efforts.

New initiatives in urban church planting and leadership training address present as well as future needs.

"Be still, and know that I am God; I will be exalted among the heathen, I will be exalted in the earth."

—Psalm 46:10

Pastor Fermin Roman and his wife, Antonia, with the Baptist Church of Mallorquin

New building at Palma Loma Church, Asunción

Ladies' get-together at the Carapachay church

Jim Evans (center right)

Ruth Greenslade with Word of Life students who helped to plant the church in Carapachay

After 20 years in Peru, Ivor and Ruth Greenslade partnered with Jim and Sharon Evans to open a new work for ABWE in Buenos Aires, one of the world's largest cities and the capital of Argentina. They arrived in early 1979 and began holding services in the Greenslades' home on Easter Sunday.

In January 1980, that church was organized with 23 charter members. Later, ABWE purchased an old theater in the suburbs of Carapachay to house the church.

"South America still needs missionaries. In the midst of religious confusion, many people are looking for the truth found only in Jesus Christ."

—David Southwell, *Message*, Summer 1999

Ruth and Ivor Greenslade

New missionary personnel gave additional impetus to the church-planting program, most of it centered in the metropolitan area. Concentration on an extensive children's ministry led to the salvation of hundreds of youth, many of them now active in local churches. A national mission board was formed in 2001.

The Argentine mission agency, "Adelfos," is introduced.

WESTERN EUROPE

EXECUTIVE ADMINISTRATORS FOR WESTERN EUROPE

William J. Hopewell

In 1977, Bill became executive administrator for Africa, Europe, and South America, and served in that capacity until 1986.

Jesse G. Eaton

Jess and Joyce served with ABWE in Bangladesh from 1964 to 1981. After several years in a Christian college, Jess was appointed to administer Western Europe in 1987. Nine years later he passed the baton to Jack Shiflett.

L. Jack Shiflett

Jack and Cheryl came to ABWE from a successful pastoral ministry and served in church planting in Spain for 15 years. In 1996, Jack was appointed executive administrator for Western Europe.

SPAIN & ENGLAND

Making inroads into society has included organizing a youth basketball program. Little by little, barriers are breaking down in this country where for so long religious intolerance was codified by law. As barriers break down, the harvest we pray for will come.

Bill Stoner preaches in a Spanish church.

After decades of being closed to Protestant missionaries, Spain's changing political climate in 1968 marked not only the opening of a door to enter the country of Spain but also ABWE's first expansion into Western Europe. Bill and Rosie Stoner transferred from Chile and were the first of numerous missionaries who helped start churches both in metropolitan Madrid and in southern regions of the country.

Three churches are approaching self-support status and two new church plants are in the early stages. ABWE operates an MK school in conjunction with four other mission agencies.

"If it be the duty of all men to believe the gospel, then it is the duty of those who are entrusted with the gospel to endeavor to make it known among all men."

—William Carey, 1786

A survey trip in 1984 highlighted the need for missionaries in England. Jim and Carol West arrived in the Bristol area in 1985 and were invited to pastor Tyndale Baptist Chapel, started almost 100 years earlier.

In 2000, two churches reached independent status, calling their own national pastors. Now the ABWE England team is beginning work "from scratch" with the support of a nearby national English church in Quedgeley. The team also is working in Swindon to start a new church there.

"Only 3% of the population attends church regularly."

—The Evangelical Times

The missionary team in England has been involved primarily in rescuing dwindling congregations of existing churches.

Holiday camps reach children

Tyndale Baptist Chapel was founded in 1890 when Charles Spurgeon sent "preacher boys" to the town of Chipping Sodbury.

NORWAY & FRANCE

Jack Slough leads a Bible study in his home.

ABWE entered Norway in 1981. The four missionary couples who work in the country today target two different groups around Oslo, the capital city. One team primarily seeks to reach Norwegians in their own language; the other works through the International Baptist Church which started in 1985.

The International Baptist Church has touched the lives of people from 90 countries, including businessmen, diplomats, and students. Embassy personnel who were believers when they came have been strengthened by the church, and witness for Christ in government circles.

"I toiled at the task [of the Institutes] chiefly for the sake of my countrymen, the French, multitudes of whom I perceived to be hungering and thirsting after Christ, while very few seemed to have been duly imbued with even a slender knowledge of Him."

—John Calvin

John and Geraldine Weeks

The Lord laid a burden for France on the hearts of a father and son team, John and Geraldine Weeks, and Tim and Marsha Weeks. The missionaries discovered that children's Bible clubs, an American football team, and mass literature distribution are effective means for spreading the gospel. The missionaries are excited about their strategy involving a family center for penetrating the spiritual darkness of Montpellier in southern France.

PORTUGAL

Lisbon Training Center

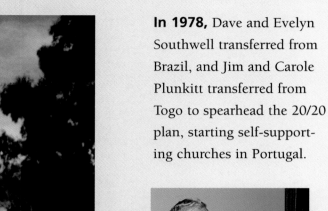

In 1978, Dave and Evelyn Southwell transferred from Brazil, and Jim and Carole Plunkitt transferred from Togo to spearhead the 20/20 plan, starting self-supporting churches in Portugal.

Jim Plunkitt

Today, with nine churches established or in formation, the Portugal missionary team has developed a new plan to reach the greater Lisbon area in the next 16 years through 16 churches. A key facet of ministry includes the Lisbon Training Center, which offers training for national leaders and also houses the MK school.

Miriam Tyers develops relationships with students in the public schools near the Training Center.

GERMANY & ITALY

With the collapse of the Iron Curtain, reunited Germany became a nation of 81.5 million. In 1990, ABWE began church-planting efforts, focusing on two target areas. Rocky and Arlene Hartung arrived in 1992 to work in Kassel, where the church called Freie Baptisten Gemeinde is located. The other area centers in Kusel, where evangelistic tent campaigns have proven effective. A mother church is led by Michael and Liselotte Landoll, and two daughter churches are being formed.

"In one sense, Germany is very religious. Public school education includes religious education classes. Over 70% of the population still claims membership in the established churches, although most limit attendance to Christmas and Easter. A closer look, however, reveals that beneath the external 'Christian' veneer, a spiritual vacuum exists. In this spiritual vacuum, ABWE missionaries are seeking to evangelize and establish vibrant, biblically focused churches."

—Ralph Gruenberg
Germany country coordinator

Rocky Hartung (right)

Una Parola per oggi

GENNAIO
2001
lunedì

1

Il Signore
disse:
Io sono con te.

Missionaries participate in a community medieval pageant.

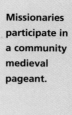

David Stevenson meets with an Italian friend.

Part of the Italy team in Avigliana

A 1988 survey reported that of Italy's 32,000 towns and cities, 31,000 had no evangelical witness of any kind! David and Rosezell Stevenson were appointed to open this field.

ABWE's ministry in Italy is located on the outskirts of the city of Turin. The team uses Bible studies, English classes, sports teams, participation in local civic groups, and literature distribution—including Scripture calendars—to enhance church planting.

In March 1996, worship services began in a hotel. The congregation grew and needed its own facilities. After two years of searching and praying, a property on the main street in town was made available. The missionaries named it *Il Faro* (The Lighthouse), a place where Italians can come for counseling, Bible studies, and fellowship.

AFRICA

Executive Administrators for Africa

William J. Hopewell
In 1977, Bill became executive administrator for Africa, Europe, and South America, and served in that capacity until 1986.

Jesse G. Eaton
Jess and Joyce served with ABWE in Bangladesh from 1964 to 1981. Jess was appointed to administer Africa in 1987.

Ronald A. Washer
Ron and Ann served in Togo from 1979 to 1994. At that time, they were invited to join the administrative team in the Harrisburg office. Ron worked first in the enlistment department and then became executive administrator for Africa in 2000.

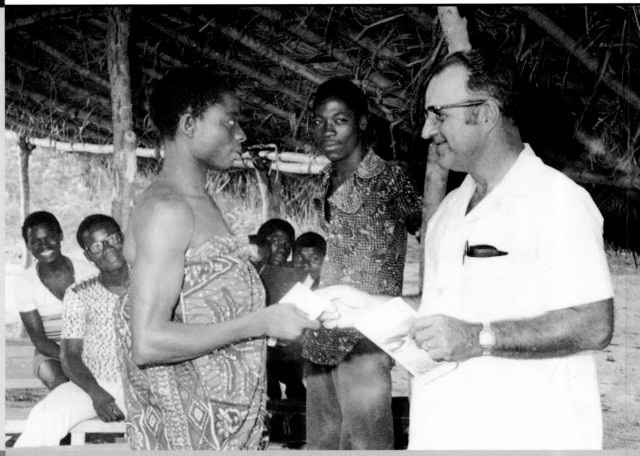

Dal Washer's first love was village evangelism.

Tim Matchett teaching

Dallas and Kay Washer, 18-year veterans of another mission agency, surveyed the countries of Benin and Togo for ABWE in 1973. They began a church-planting ministry in Lomé, the capital city of Togo, with Dave and Elwanda Fields. Receptivity to the gospel resulted in the start-up of two churches.

When more co-workers joined the team, the Washers moved into the interior. There they developed the Blind Center along with a church-planting initiative. In 1985 the construction of the Karolyn Kempton Memorial Christian Hospital established medical ministry under doctors Dave Clutts and Bob Cropsey. The hospital serves as another church-planting center near the village of Tsiko. Literacy and translation work take place at the Resource Center there and in northern Togo, where missionaries began outreach in 1986.

Ndungu Kebbeh nursery school

After serving in the Niger Republic, Melvin and Ruby Pittman joined ABWE to develop a ministry in The Gambia. In 1978, the Pittmans opened a mission post in Ndungu Kebbeh, which quickly became a medical station utilizing Ruby's nursing skills and those of Ruth Wood, who joined them in 1980. Short-term personnel helped maintain this beachhead in the predominately Muslim region for several years.

Career mission-aries expanded the medical ministry to include a 20-bed clinic, a literature and literacy center, and a nursery school as methods for sharing the gospel.

Deb Haegert teaches a Bible lesson.

Ruth Wood, a mainstay of ABWE's work in The Gambia

South African
believers
involved in
local outreach

Coach Bobby Hile at
a city-wide basketball
tournament

God again used a veteran missionary couple, Marc and Judie Blackwell, who were joined by Dale and Karen Marshfield to develop church planting and leadership training in the large city of Durban. The Baptist Bible College of Natal trains men and women to help with church planting in and around the city. A growing youth program reaches the large population of young people. Through the Blessing Durban Fund, three of the nine established churches now have their own buildings.

Dale Marshfield (left)
mentors local
pastor Vic Willis.

"Working as a team to build churches that are actively reaching the world."

—Dale Marshfield from *Blessing Durban* brochure

As the missionary team continued to grow, reaching Afrikaaners in Cape Town weighed heavily on the Blackwells. They opened the Church Ministries Institute to train and mentor men for leadership in the local churches being started. God has broadened the original vision to include Good Hope Christian School and the Paardeberg Mountain Retreat and Camp.

Sunday School at Community Baptist Church

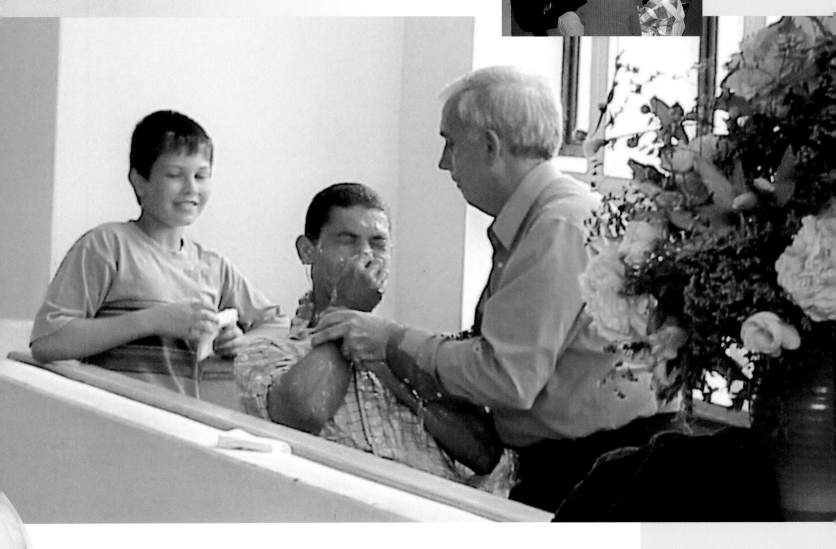

Marc Blackwell, Sr., baptizes a man led to Christ by a CMI student.

KENYA, GHANA, LIBERIA, & BENIN

Students from Mathetes Bible College in Ghana

Believers from Togo churches who live across the border in Ghana encouraged ABWE missionaries to start a church in the Volta Region of Ghana. Bob and Lois Dyer pioneered church planting and Mathetes Bible College in the town of Ho, Volta Region. Veteran missionaries from other fields joined the team to continue building on the Dyers' foundation.

Dave Fields and Terry Washer with a Kikuyu tribal group in Kenya

Dave and Elwanda Fields transferred from Togo in 1983 to open Kenya to ABWE church planting. After several years of witnessing and discipleship, God is raising up national leaders from Grace Baptist Church to work with the missionaries. Together with these leaders, Russ and Barbara Stockman envision reaching people through a community center.

Bob Dyer gathers a nucleus of believers in Ghana.

Medical Clinic in Bonga, Liberia

During Liberia's seven-year civil war, Christians fled to other West African countries. Two men attended the Mathetes Bible College in Ghana and invited ABWE to partner with the African Fundamental Baptist Mission. An ABWE missionary team is forming to initiate the on-site partnership, which will include theological training and church planting through medical clinics, Christian school development, and agricultural assistance for local evangelists.

Tim and Helen Matchett, missionaries in Togo, talked about moving 100 miles east to assist several churches at their invitation in Cotonou, Benin, with leadership training and church planting. In October 1999, Tim was killed, but the vision remained. Because of the proximity to Togo, missionaries in Benin benefit from the pool of experienced missionaries serving across the border.

Jane Schmitz trains women in Bible teaching.

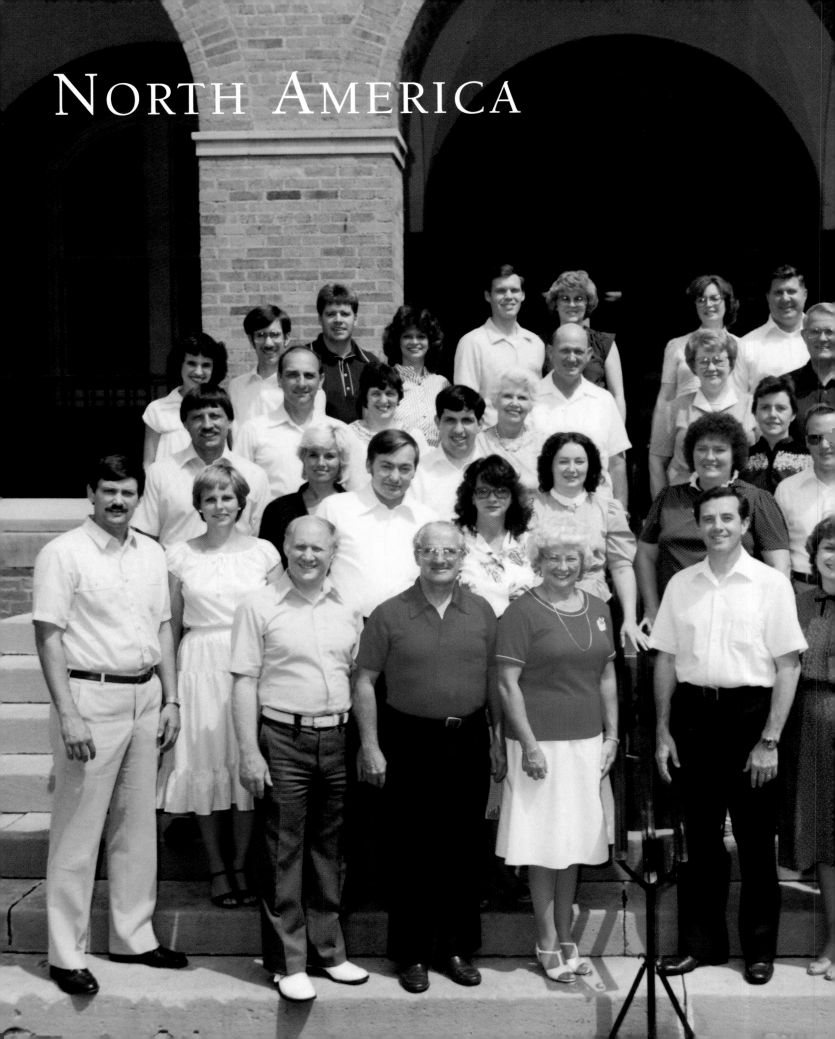

NORTH AMERICA

Executive Administrators for North America

Floyd A. Davis

Floyd and Gayle joined ABWE in 1976 after 30 years of pastoral and leadership experience. The board asked Floyd to launch the ABWE-USA ministry. He provided inspirational leadership until his battle with cancer claimed his life on July 4, 1982.

Norman A. Nicklas

Norm and Evelyn started four churches during their three terms in São Paulo, Brazil. After Floyd Davis' death, Norm was called to lead the church-planting ministry in North America, which included Mexico City until that city passed to the administrator of Central America and the Caribbean in 2001.

UNITED STATES

Current facility of Faith Baptist Church, Winter Haven, Florida

On April 13, 1976, the ABWE board opened the USA as its newest field in order to plant churches and raise up new missionaries.

Church Planting: One of the first two USA missionary couples, Willard and Donna Benedict, served in Bangladesh before returning to the States for health reasons. They started Faith Baptist Church in Winter Haven, Florida. The second couple, Bob and Lois Dyer, returned from Papua New Guinea and started Shawnee Baptist Church in Shamong, New Jersey.

Sam and Darlene Farlow established churches in three different states; Dave and Cherri Cooper established two churches in Massachusetts; and Earl and Marilyn Shaffer started three churches in Ohio.

CHURCH TO CHURCH IN USA • 1977–2001

19 States • 38 Churches • 15 Church Strengthenings

Over **50 full-time workers** have been raised up by ABWE–USA churches!

Church planting provides laborers for the harvest field!

ABWE

Over **6 Million Dollars** has been given by ABWE—USA churches to ABWE since 1989!

$6,468,752

Church planting provides money to support our ABWE missionaries!

Over **250 missionaries** are supported by ABWE–USA churches!

Church planting provides funds to support missionaries from other boards!

Terry Armstrong, Robert Velasquez, and Norm Nicklas

Sam Farlow's men's sports outreach at Westwood Baptist Church, Fresno, California

Church Strengthening: In addition to starting churches, ABWE missionaries help struggling churches grow. As a result of this church-strengthening program, churches in Arizona, Florida, New Jersey, and Oregon are now effectively reaching their communities.

Churches Among Ethnic Populations: Congregations among ethnic populations such as Hispanics and Laotians have led to missionaries who now serve overseas.

Linhthong Phrasavath

CANADA

A bar was converted to house the
Vermilyeas' church.

The Billingtons and the Vermilyeas

Canadian missionary
Ivor Greenslade made a
special appeal to open his
homeland to church plant-
ing. Supervision of the
missionaries working in
Canada is under the joint
leadership of the Canadian
Council of ABWE and the
executive administrator for
North America.

Quebec province
represents more than seven
million French-speaking
Canadians.

In 1990, Tim and Barb
Vermilyea began Bible studies in Port-Rouge, west of
Quebec City. The growing
group moved into rented
facilities, and then into its
own property in the center
of town in 1999.

In 1990, Gary and
Debbie Manter transferred
from Portugal to work with
English- and Portuguese-
speaking communities in
Ontario, helping to develop
Faith Baptist Church in
Kitchener and bring it to
self-support.

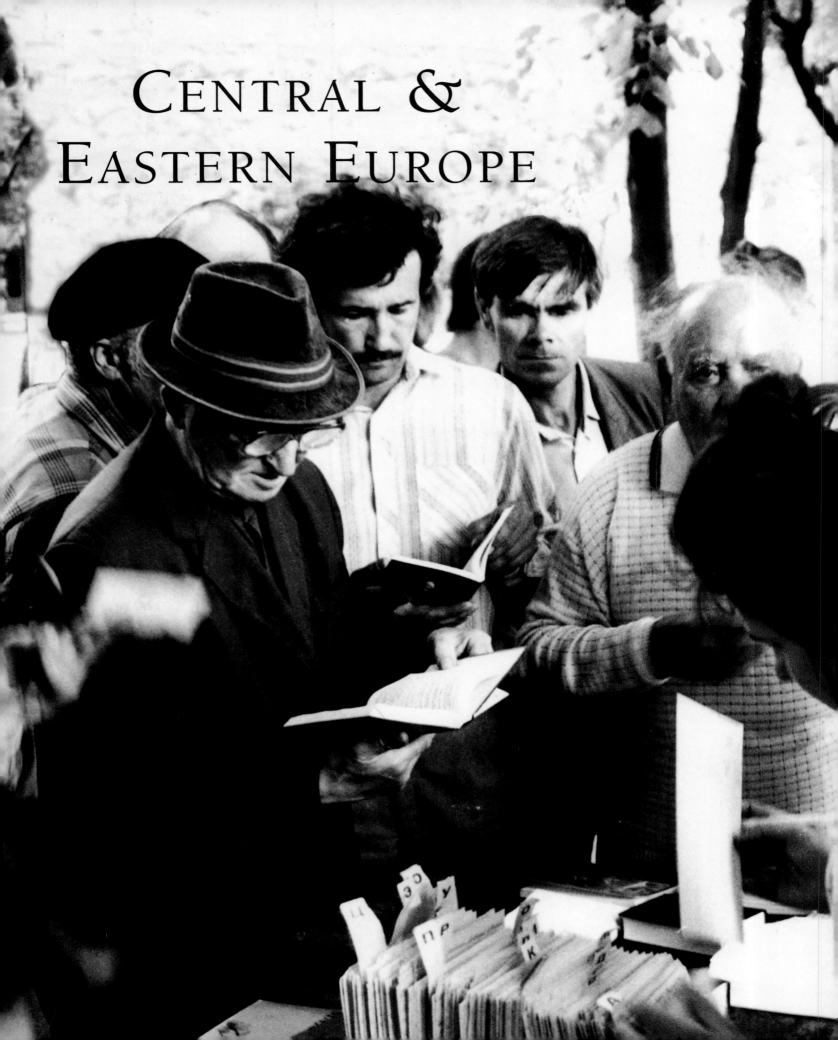

CENTRAL & EASTERN EUROPE

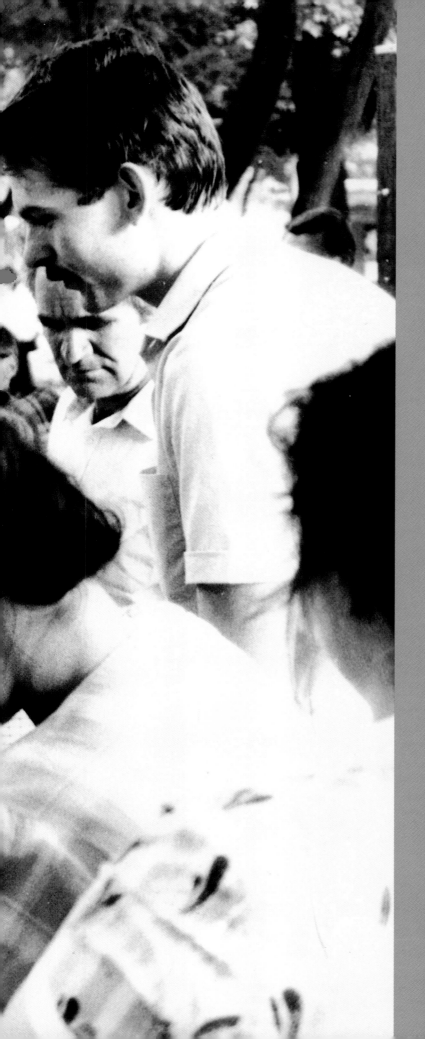

EXECUTIVE ADMINISTRATORS FOR CENTRAL & EASTERN EUROPE

Michael G. Loftis
Michael and Jo Beth came to ABWE from 14 years of seminary teaching and church ministries to launch the Central & Eastern Europe field in 1988. Michael served as executive administrator until his appointment as president of ABWE in 2001.

Duane M. Early
For 13 years, Duane and Sue served in pastoral positions in three churches before joining ABWE as missionaries to Ukraine. Duane succeeded Michael as administrator of this region in 2001.

HUNGARY & ROMANIA

Early ministries in cooperation with visionary Hungarian pastor Geza Kovacs led to partnership with ABWE missionaries in 1988–1989. Brian and Dianna Nester moved their family to Budapest in 1990. The next decade produced a strong nucleus of missionaries, and the Hungary team branched out from the capital city with innovative evangelistic methods and solid leadership training. One of the most effective programs has been the summer seminars for English as a second language.

Geza Kovacs, Tibor Kulcsar, Wendell Kempton, Ildiko Kovacs, Dianna and Brian Nester

"O praise the Lord, all ye nations."
—Psalm 117:1

From the first contacts with Romanian pastors suffering under the strict regime of dictator Nicolai Ceaucescu, ABWE's work in Romania gradually broadened to reach isolated villages, train pastors, and facilitate church-planting movements.

Marty and Linda Vidal became the first resident missionaries in 1993. Several more families followed the call to Romania over the next ten years.

UKRAINE & RUSSIA

**Church Ministries
Institute building**

Before the collapse of the Soviet Union, ABWE pioneered missions work among the persecuted churches of Russia and Ukraine. The Kemptons, along with missionaries Ivor and Ruth Greenslade and Larry and Jacqui Armstrong, led the way for a young, vibrant team of resident missionaries to begin evangelism and church planting in the early 1990s. Scott and Lisa Carter arrived in Odessa in 1992, followed by John and Jacky Taylor in 1993. Scores of volunteers answered the challenge to help construct the Church Ministries Institute in Odessa, with further leadership training centers and church plants in Kiev and Kharkov. Evangelistic thrusts such as "Bibles to Russia," village medical clinics, and family camps enhance the ongoing ministries in Ukraine.

Scott Carter, Wendell Kempton, Duane Early

> *"God did not always promise to protect us, but He did promise to produce fruit through us."*
>
> —Michael Loftis

**Church Ministries
Institute student group**

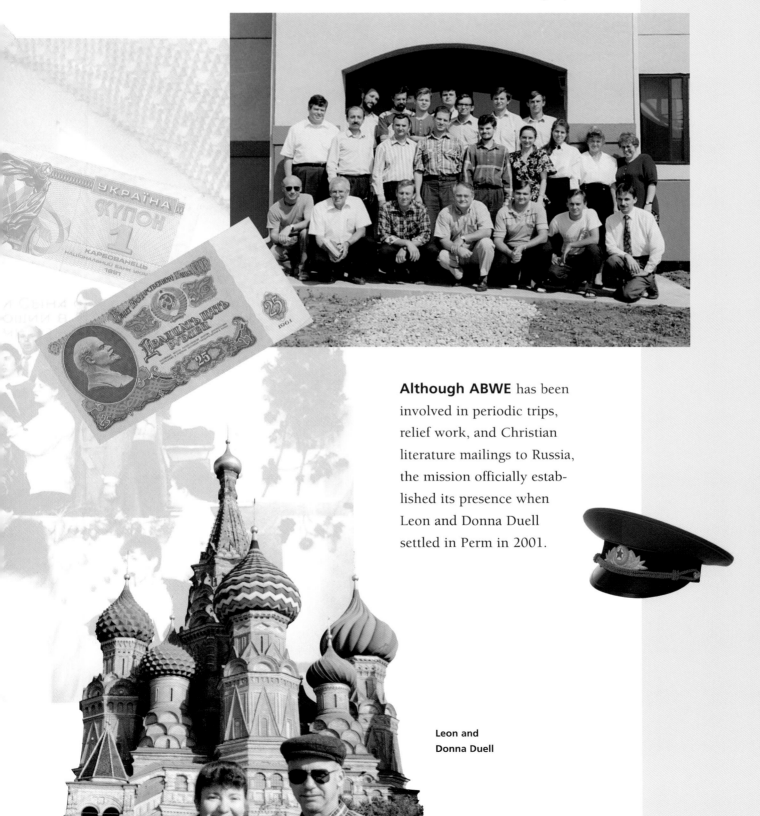

Although ABWE has been involved in periodic trips, relief work, and Christian literature mailings to Russia, the mission officially established its presence when Leon and Donna Duell settled in Perm in 2001.

**Leon and
Donna Duell**

BOSNIA, CROATIA, & SLOVAKIA

Arriving in Slovakia in 1996, Don and Cherry Eade immediately began recruiting a team of coworkers while simultaneously strengthening fledgling Slovak churches.

The void left by years of communist oppression provided numerous opportunities for outreach and training among all age groups.

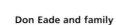

Don Eade and family

**Mark Nikitin,
Wendell Kempton,
Michael Loftis**

Relief efforts and leadership training throughout the war-torn Balkans began in the mid 1990s as the Central and Eastern European Regional Team began offering church workers' seminars along with humanitarian aid and mercy ministries. Mark Nikitin and Larry Haag coordinate regular assistance to Baptist churches in Bosnia and Croatia, developing strong partnerships with young pastors.

Larry and Sharon Haag

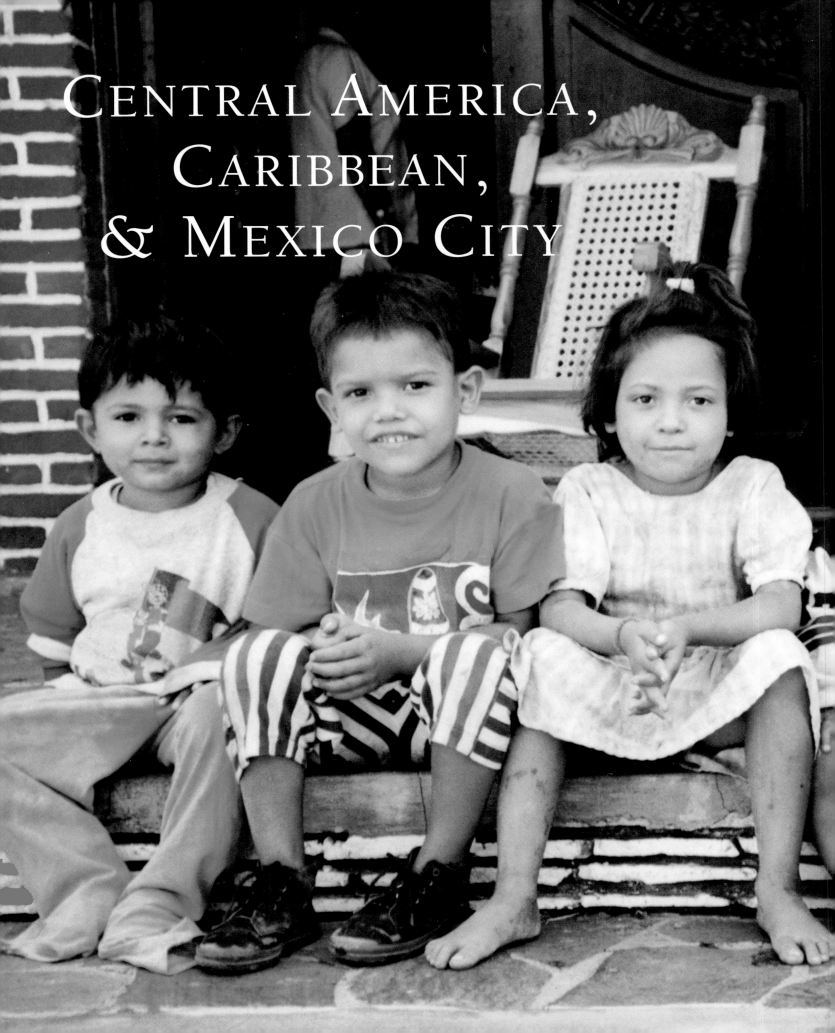

CENTRAL AMERICA,
CARIBBEAN,
& MEXICO CITY

EXECUTIVE ADMINISTRATORS FOR CENTRAL AMERICA, CARIBBEAN, & MEXICO CITY

Dan Gelatt, Jr.

Dan and Cindy served as church planters in Argentina before being invited to open a new region of ministry for ABWE in Central America and the Caribbean in 1993. Dan pioneered this work until cancer took Cindy to heaven in 1996.

Larry D. Smith

Larry and Beverly began their service with ABWE in 1964, first in Chile, then in Mexico City. From 1992 to 1996, Larry served as missions professor at Heritage Baptist College and Seminary in Canada before assuming leadership of Central America and the Caribbean, which now includes Mexico City.

Since 1995 Larry and Bev Smith have taught in a seminary and preached in churches in Cuba. The Smiths also administrate the Cuban Book Project, which supplies mini-libraries for Cuban pastors. Along with the Smiths, two other couples serve as non-residential missionaries to Cuba.

A group of 27 Baptist churches in Trinidad and Tobago asked that ABWE missionaries help train their pastors. Tim and Jane Bahula and Dennis and Bonnie Slothower will be involved in theological training and church-strengthening ministries there.

Larry and Bev Smith began teaching seminars in Nicaragua several months before Hurricane Mitch struck in 1998. Dubbed "the worst storm in two centuries," the hurricane resulted in an estimated loss of 11,000 lives. The Smiths distributed $85,000 worth of relief supplies donated by Christians in North America.

Because of the Smiths' involvement, local Christians asked for additional theological training. This, along with church planting and strengthening, will be the major focus of the ABWE team in Nicaragua. Andy and Diane Large transferred from Peru to begin a church among the professional class in the capital city of Managua, while Mark and Diane Henzler transfered from Chile to emphasize pastoral leadership training and theological education.

Paul and Patty Collier served in Paraguay for 20 years when the Lord directed them to church planting in Costa Rica. They arrived in 1999 to work among professionals and students, with the goal of raising up a network of strong churches. LaMar and Joanna Salley are involved in a new church plant in San José, the capital city.

MEXICO CITY

The Navarrete family

The ABWE board voted in 1987 to open a work in Mexico City, the largest city in the world, with more than 23 million people. Larry and Bev Smith transferred from Chile to start the work, and were joined by Paul and Susie Hardy, who transferred from Spain. Both the Smiths and the Hardys were forced to leave because of medical conditions brought on by the city's severe pollution and the high altitude.

The Hardys had established Missionary Baptist Church in a growing middle-class suburb. Pastors of other congregations assisted the church until ABWE missionaries, Antonio and Diana Navarrete, arrived in December 2000. The church is growing and a daughter congregation is under way.

10th Anniversary of Iglesia Bautista Misionera

(Right) Mexico City, the world's largest city, under its perpetual cloud of pollution

"Remember, when you see a missionary coming home broken in body and weary in soul, it isn't the privations or dangers or things he's <u>done</u> that leave a deep hurt; it's the things he <u>couldn't</u> do that break his heart."

—Anonymous

RESTRICTED ACCESS

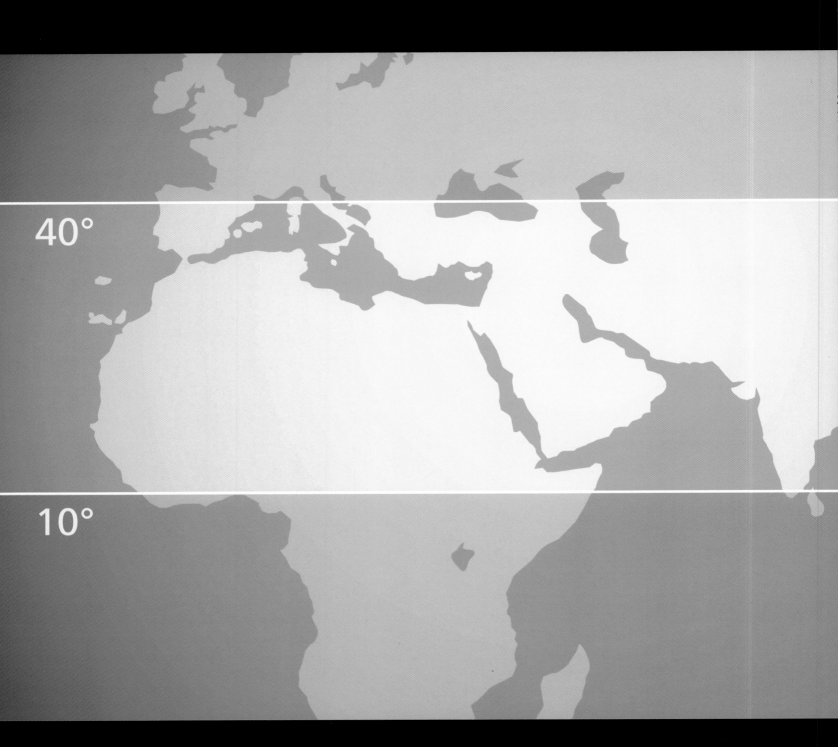

40°

10°

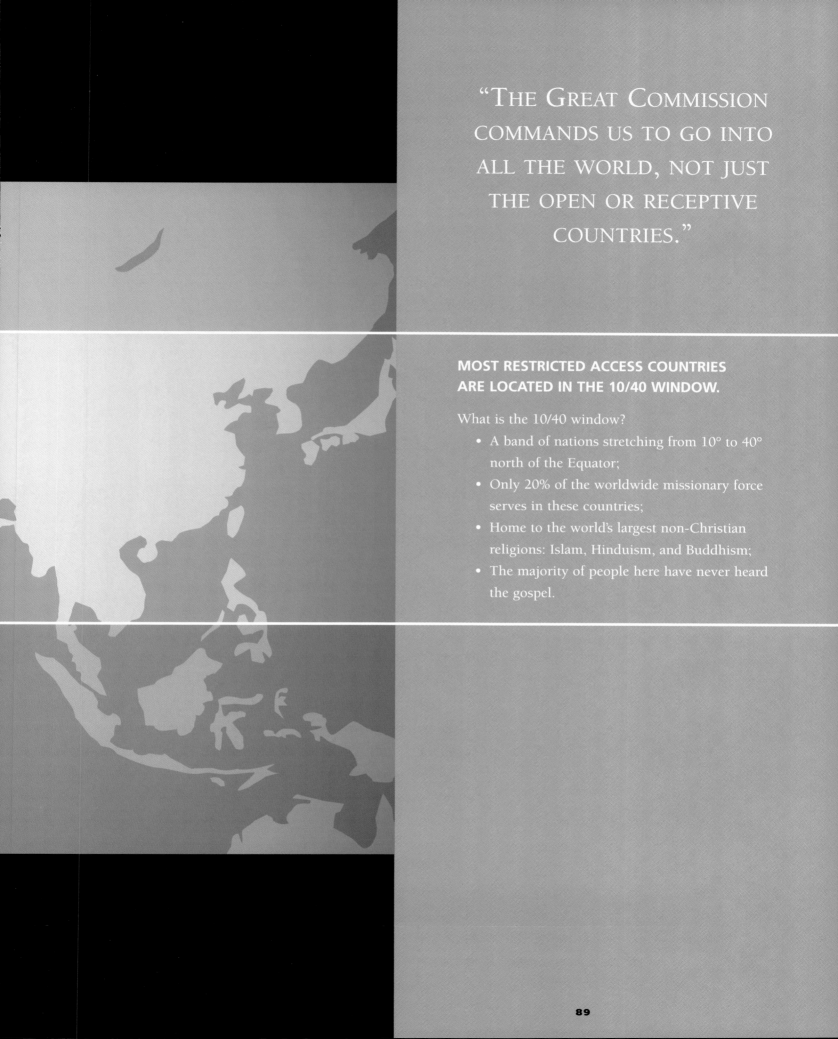

"THE GREAT COMMISSION COMMANDS US TO GO INTO ALL THE WORLD, NOT JUST THE OPEN OR RECEPTIVE COUNTRIES."

MOST RESTRICTED ACCESS COUNTRIES ARE LOCATED IN THE 10/40 WINDOW.

What is the 10/40 window?

- A band of nations stretching from 10° to 40° north of the Equator;
- Only 20% of the worldwide missionary force serves in these countries;
- Home to the world's largest non-Christian religions: Islam, Hinduism, and Buddhism;
- The majority of people here have never heard the gospel.

WIN, GAP, & GLOBAL NEIGHBORS

WIN—winning the window: The ABWE board in 1995 unanimously approved the creation of WIN, a family of humanitarian and business ventures. WIN places missionaries in secular organizations in order to share the gospel discreetly in countries of the persecuted church.

Workers in restricted access countries have secular credentials and experience as well as ministry training. This allows them to provide valued services while creating contacts and building relationships with those who desperately need Christ in unreached corners of the world.

Partnership at work in Nepal

Better known by its acronym **GAP, Global Access Partnerships** stands in the GAP historically at a transition period when many countries in the world restrict missionary access. At the same time, an increasing number of missionaries are coming from non-Western countries. In order to reach restricted access nations with the gospel message, strategic partnerships with godly and like-minded friends overseas is an increasing necessity.

Some GAP projects include sponsoring evangelistic training seminars among tribal groups in Southeast Asia and purchasing equipment for national evangelists and pastors.

Global Neighbors was incorporated in 1996 as a non-government organization (NGO) to facilitate ministries in restricted access countries. Global Neighbors is a corporate identity through which ABWE personnel function in specific countries, enabling them to have a presence in parts of the world otherwise inaccessible to missionaries.

Grace Baptist boarding facility in northern Thailand

"To one
of the
least of
these"

SPECIALIZED

MINISTRIES

OPENING DOORS FOR EVANGELISM

MEDICAL EVANGELISM

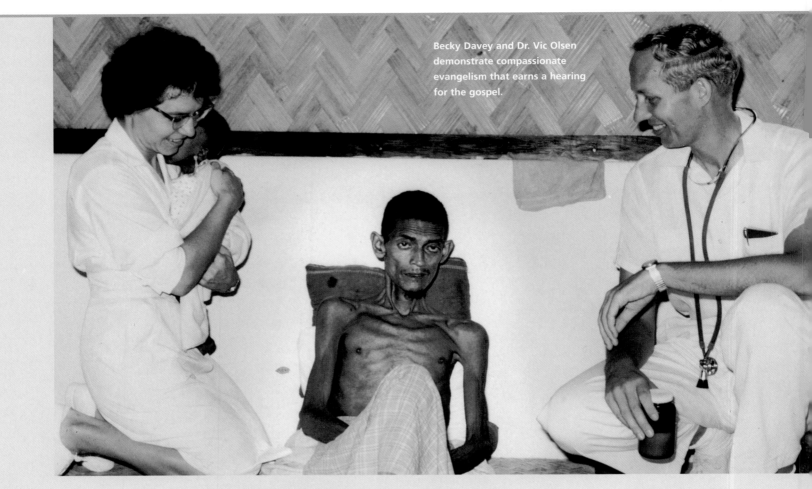

Becky Davey and Dr. Vic Olsen demonstrate compassionate evangelism that earns a hearing for the gospel.

In the Philippines nurses Rhoda Little and Gladys DeVries opened a clinic in Mindanao. Under the direction of doctor-and-nurse team Link and Lenore Nelson, the clinic evolved into the Bethel Baptist Hospital in 1955.

ABWE began three other hospitals now under local administrators and staff:

- Leyte Baptist Hospital
- Palawan Baptist Hospital
- Aklan Baptist Hospital

More than 800 churches have been established throughout the Philippines as a result of medical evangelism.

Dr. Link and Lenore Nelson founded ABWE hospitals in the Philippines and, since retirement, have filled in at every other ABWE medical facility.

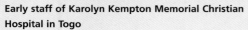

Early staff of Karolyn Kempton Memorial Christian Hospital in Togo

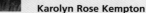

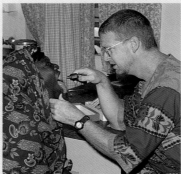

Karolyn Rose Kempton

God used the deaths of 14-year-old Mary Barnard and translator Paul Miller in East Pakistan (now **Bangladesh**) to prompt Dr. Viggo and Joan Olsen to gather a team for Memorial Christian Hospital, dedicated on March 25, 1966. The hospital helps to meet the medical needs of more than ten million Bangladeshis, and is instrumental in reaching many for Christ.

Compassionate medical care opens doors for the gospel in **The Gambia**, where it is not possible to preach openly. Ruby Pittman, Ruth Wood, and an array of short- and long-term medical personnel ran a clinic from 1981 until the Ndungu Kebbeh Health Centre opened in 1989.

Kevin Johnson, The Gambia

The initial building of Amazonas Baptist Hospital in Santo Antonio do Iça, **Brazil**, was dedicated in 1985 under the leadership of Dr. Jack and Sandy Sorg. An addition was opened in February 1998.

The Karolyn Kempton Memorial Christian Hospital in **Togo** opened in 1985. July 10, 1999, marked graduation day for the first class in a nurses' training program.

Mobile medical clinics

organized and conducted by Dr. Miriam Wheeler and nurse practitioner Dr. Sharon Rahilly enable pastors in **Ukraine** to take the gospel to more than 100 villages.

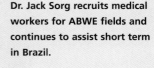

Dr. Jack Sorg recruits medical workers for ABWE fields and continues to assist short term in Brazil.

Gladys DeVries, Philippines, ca. 1930

BIBLE TRANSLATION

After a six-week course in translation principles, exegesis, and linguistic analysis, Virginia DeVries (right) spent 15 years with Teodoro and Balbina Abadiano translating the Scriptures into Cuyonon.

ABWE's first Bible translation work was in Cuyonon, the mother tongue of about 200,000 people in the Palawan province of the **Philippines**. The New Testament was published in 1977.

After 32 years of translating and formatting in **Bangladesh**, the Standard Bengali Common Language Bible was finally available in 1995. Using that work as a base, Vic and Joan Olsen and local translators prepared the Muslim Bengali Common Language New Testament. George King brought the full Bible to completion in 2000. The Standard Bengali Common Language also served as the base in translating the New Testament into four tribal languages under the supervision of Jay Walsh, Vicki Shaw, Annette Shiley, Harold Ebersole, and Phil Walsh.

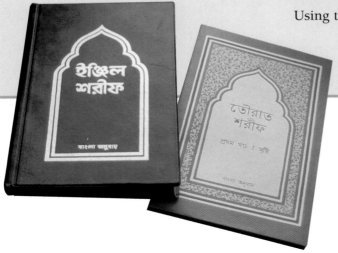

Injil Sharif (New Testament)
and *Towrat Sharif* (Pentateuch)

"Car Dieu a tant aimé le monde qu'il a donné son Fils unique, afin que quiconque croit en lui ne périsse point, mais qu'il ait la vie éternelle." (Jean 3:16)

—John 3:16, in French

"As I began my missionary work in **Togo**," wrote Vicki Shaw, "I had nothing in the tribal languages most people speak." What began as a simple plan to provide materials for local churches mushroomed into a network of ministries throughout Togo and **Ghana**.

Vicki (Shaw) Ivester works with a Togolese woman to translate Bible lessons in West Africa.

Lynn Silvernale (far left) worked with other missionaries in a verse-by-verse exegesis of Scripture in Bangladesh. Of the seven Bangladeshis who worked on translation, Mrs. Basanti Das (second from left) was the main translator for the entire Bible.

LITERACY & LITERATURE

ABWE missionaries in many countries established literacy classes to assist children and adults in reading and writing their own languages. Since much of the curriculum is from the Bible, learning to read also means learning about God's love shown through Jesus Christ.

A Gambian facilitator demonstrates language learning during an International Literacy Day celebration.

Mrs. Prashona Biswas (right) and Jeannie Lockerbie working in the Literature Division in Chittagong, Bangladesh, that became the world's largest producer of Christian literature in Bengali.

Under the direction of Harry Buerer and George Haberer in the **Philippines**, ABWE operated a press, printing Sunday school and VBS materials, tracts, and songbooks in both English and Filipino languages.

In 1958, Mel Cuthbert became co-director of Editora Baptista Regular (Regular Baptist Publica-tions) in **Brazil**. For nearly 30 years, Jackson and Thelma Moore worked to produce quality Christian literature used locally and overseas.

In 1969, Jeannie Lockerbie and John Sircar opened the Literature Division in Chittagong, **East Pakistan**, to produce Christian literature in Bengali, which was then the world's sixth most spoken language. A national litera-ture board was formed in 1992 and a national manag-er installed in 2001.

La Palabra Viva (The Living Word) Bible Correspondence School (BCS) in Santiago, **Chile**, and the BCS in **Paraguay** have changed the lives of many South Americans.

ABWE and Baptist Mid-Missions' joint venture produced literature in Brazil that was sent to Portuguese-speaking people all over the world.

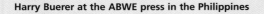

Harry Buerer at the ABWE press in the Philippines

Christian literature: a life-changing medium

AVIATION

Plane on the Togo airstrip

Pilot Tim Gainey with Wendell Kempton in Papua New Guinea

In 1958, ABWE asked Hank Scheltema to initiate an airplane ministry in Amazonas, **Brazil**. Hank and his wife, Ruth, arrived in February 1961, operating a floatplane.

Don Fanning opened the aviation work in **Colombia** in 1971. He and Butch Jarvis reached Colombians and Yucuna Indians until guerrilla activity forced this aviation ministry to close in 1984.

Larry Holman arrived in Malaybalay, **Philippines**, in 1975, then moved to Palawan a year later to start a second aviation ministry with Harry Rodgers. The cost of maintaining private aircraft eventually closed the aviation work.

In 1980, Dale and Bev Fogg began flying to the interior in **Paraguay**, where several churches have been planted.

Hank Scheltema was appointed director of aviation in 1981 to coordinate the logistics involved with acquiring and operating mission aircraft. Herman Teachout now serves as his understudy.

**Damaged propeller
blade from downed
floatplane**

Kevin Donaldson, an MK from **Peru**, arrived in Iquitos in 1987 to lay the groundwork for aviation church planting. On April 20, 2001, the mission floatplane was shot down, killing missionary Roni Bowers and seven-month-old Charity, and seriously injuring Kevin. Since 1988, Glenn Budd has flown into Andean Mountain towns, teaching and training Peruvian lay pastors.

Randy Alderman started the aviation program in **Togo** in 1989. With the help of Togolese pastors, he planted churches in and around the city of Kara.

Steve and Sandy Aholt arrived in **Papua New Guinea** in 1994 to take the gospel into remote mountainous areas. They planted a growing church in Bundi. Tim and Rebekah Gainey arrived in 1999 to partner in this ministry.

**Terry Bowers and Hank Scheltema with a
floatplane, Brazil 1969**

Larry Golin and Dr. John Bullock established the Limb and Brace Center in Bangladesh to help amputees. Pictured below, Larry holds camps where participants learn how to use a prosthesis while also learning of Jesus Christ.

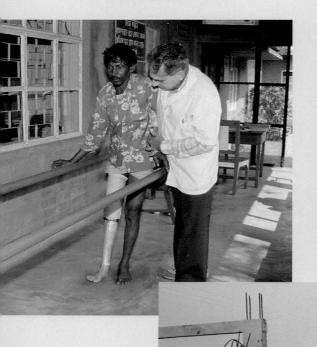

In the wake of earthquakes, hurricanes, and floods, ABWE missionaries distribute relief aid, providing another means to present the gospel.

Ruth Kempton's burden to distribute Bibles to the people of the former **Soviet Union** also generated the collection and distribution of 12 containers of food, clothing, and medical supplies.

New life in Lima—rescuing the perishing

Kay Washer founded Village of Light Blind Center in **Togo** in 1974, where hundreds have received an education and learned a useful trade. Work among the hearing-impaired takes place in **Japan**, **Brazil**, and **Peru**.

In 1997, Evelyn Stone and a Christian doctor in **Peru** envisioned a crisis pregnancy center offering biblical and medical counsel. With a team of committed local Christians reaching out to help save eternal and physical lives, New Life Pre-natal Center opened its doors on January 1, 1999.

In 1999 Kay Washer received one of Togo's highest honors, the Ordre de Mono, in recognition for the hundreds of blind people educated and trained at the school she founded.

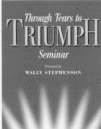

Lynn Porter (left) teaches a Bible study using sign language in Iquitos, Peru.

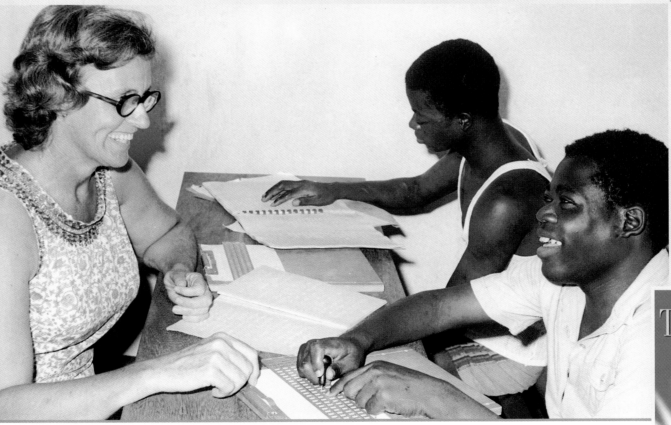

After the deaths of his wife and daughter, Wally Stephenson wrote *Through Tears to Triumph*. Wally was appointed in 1996 as director of compassionate ministries. He conducts seminars to help people cope with various kinds of grief and loss.

Through Tears to TRIUMPH *Seminar*

Presented by
WALLY STEPHENSON

Helping Hurting People

Death of a spouse, child, or friend
Separation and divorce • Wayward child or friend
Loss of health • Disability or disfigurement
Loss of independence due to aging or disease
Death of a dream • Loss of job, business, or profession
Financial troubles or bankruptcy • Moral failure
Loss of valuables or home • Suicide or murder
Miscarriage or infertility • Damaged reputation
Broken relationships

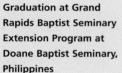

Since 1983, ABWE missionaries have been associated with Grand Rapids Baptist Seminary Extension Program and Asia Baptist Theological Seminary (GRBSEP/ABTS).

Norm and Louise Barnard and Bob and Esther Howder direct the program and manage the office work generated by 200 students in 19 countries. In the first 15 years of its existence, 93 men and women received master's degrees.

In November 1996, the International Baptist University of Theological Studies (IBU) was born in Buenos Aires, **Argentina**, to increase the level of theological training for local church leaders.

Dr. John White was invited to serve as consultant during the school's formative years and eventually became the university's president. Missionary Allan Cuthbert serves as vice president.

Graduation at Grand Rapids Baptist Seminary Extension Program at Doane Baptist Seminary, Philippines

Like father, like son: Mel Cuthbert was involved in ABWE's seminary in São Paulo, Brazil, and his son, Allan, serves as vice president of the International Baptist University.

Bob Howder with a student in Myanmar

INTERNATIONAL MINISTRIES

Larry Armstrong directs two Pastors' Consultations each year to help pastors gain a vision for effective involvement of their churches in missions.

George and Debra Collins

George and Debra Collins were missionaries in Bangladesh for 14 years before launching GAP (Global Access Partnerships). In addition, George was appointed in 2001 as director of international ministries, a group of experienced special assignment consultants who form a rich resource to assist in:

- Theological education
- Church development
- Outreach to Muslims
- Children's ministries
- MK education
- Medical education and consultation

Anna Ruth Hille in the MK Education Resource Room at ABWE, Harrisburg

CHINESE MINISTRIES WORLDWIDE

"I realize the baton has now shifted to us who were led to Christ and trained by foreign missionaries."
—Po Wan Yeung

Rev. Po Wan Yeung, director of international Chinese ministries, was one of only two full-time students in the new Hong Kong Baptist Bible Institute in 1966, and was among the first to graduate. Later he and an ABWE missionary teamed up to plant a church in Kwai Shing, where Po Wan eventually became pastor. That was the start of an outstanding career as a church planter and pastor, first in Hong Kong, then in Toronto, Canada.

Now Po Wan and Miranda Yeung travel to many countries as they challenge churches to send missionaries to the vast multitudes of Chinese who have yet to hear of Christ.

Po Wan Yeung studies diligently at Hong Kong Baptist Bible Institute (1966).

"If North Americans have such love for the Chinese people, why don't
we Chinese tell our own people? That is what we want to do."
—Miranda Yeung

"Fellow
helpers
to the
truth"

ADMINISTRATION

ADMINISTRATION

FIVE ADMINISTRATIVE DIVISIONS LINKING
SUPPORTING CHURCHES AND MISSION FIELDS

Standing: Jo Beth and Michael Loftis, Lois Cunninghame, Barbara Shuff
Seated: Elsie Miller, Jean Shawver

Diligent men and women in ABWE's corporate offices hold the ropes for the field teams. Faithful administrative assistants in the president's office dedicate themselves to filling vital roles.

Entire office personnel, 1994

The following areas come directly under the purview of the ABWE president:

PRAYER

Upon returning to the United States from Australia, John Koster began his work as the international director of world prayer in 1995. John gathers prayer requests from around the world and distributes them to the ABWE family and prayer warriors in North America.

PACE

The acronym PACE stands for People Advancing Compassionate Evangelism. In 1979, Wendell Kempton, Bill Pierson, and Jay Walsh designed this program to provide income for special projects such as:

- Helping purchase the Paardeberg Mountain Retreat in Cape Town, South Africa;
- Helping the Chia church in Bogotá, Colombia, purchase land;
- Providing water storage tanks for the Bible College in Goroka, Papua New Guinea.

Almost every ABWE field has benefited from PACE.

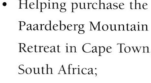

Elsie Miller, secretary to Harold Commons and Wendell Kempton, still volunteers several days a week in the president's office.

Dolores Franz, secretary to Wendell Kempton since 1993

INTERNATIONAL MEDICAL DIRECTOR

In October 1968, **Dr. Warren Bibighaus** became the medical advisor for ABWE and medical consultant for the candidate program. "Dr. B.", as he is affectionately called, served in this capacity for 20 years.

Dr. Richard and Carol Stagg served in Bangladesh from 1973 until 1988, when they returned to the United States. Dr. Stagg was appointed international medical director in 1993.

Back row: Ron Washer, Amber Joy Huey, Po Wan Yeung, Jack Shiflett, Emily Kulp, Debbie Heritage, Kent Craig
Middle row: Phil and Barb Klumpp, Pat Henry, Norm Nicklas, Dave Southwell, Jess Eaton
Seated: Carol Bibighaus, Georgia Jovich, George Collins, Bill Commons, Julianne Beard
Not pictured: Duane Early, Russ Ebersole, Beth Isbell, Larry Smith

MISSIONARY ADMINISTRATION DIVISION

This division is composed of all regional administrators and others involved in overseeing missionary personnel.

Russ and Nancy Ebersole (right) debriefing the McClures

For 15 years, Russ Ebersole was chairman of this division, followed by Bill Commons and now George Collins. In addition to overseeing missionary work around the world, this division also includes the following specialized areas:

MISSIONARY CARE

Missionary care begins during the application process and continues throughout the missionaries' active ministry and into retirement. Personnel offer consultation on health, MK education, strategy planning, and coping with grief. By every means possible, ABWE seeks to tangibly express personal care for its missionary family.

POST-FIELD INTERPERSONAL MINISTRIES (PIM)

Bill and Ruth Large, who served in Peru for more than 30 years, started a program for retired ABWE missionaries. In 1992, this was extended to include all ABWE career missionaries and office personnel who were no longer active in ministry with ABWE.

SINGLES MINISTRY

Mary Lou Brownell served for 30 years in Bangladesh until 1986 when she entered a new ministry as executive coordinator of singles ministries. Mary Lou served until her retirement in 1993. Carol Bibighaus assumed the directorship of the singles ministry after serving in Hong Kong for 20 years. ABWE has 114 single career missionaries who assist in church planting, discipleship, and Christian education; 36% of them are also involved in compassionate ministries.

Frank and Doris Jertberg (below) were the first directors of PIM. **Jesse and Joyce Eaton** assumed the leadership in 2000. PIM serves as an "alumni association" for the worldwide ABWE family.

"Who says it's no fun being a missionary?" Carol Bibighaus and her gang at a North Carolina retreat

Standing: Loren and Barbara Andersen, Don Trott, Paul and Kathy Holritz
Seated: Linda Morgan, Bill Dooley, Jennifer Wehry
Not pictured: Rick Caynor, Kay Wharton

ENLISTMENT & PRE-FIELD DIVISION

This division oversees the recruitment and screening of new missionaries, coaching and encouraging new appointees in their pre-field experience.

Donald Moffat became the first deputation director in October 1944, assisted by Bob Burns. Harold Amstutz became candidate and deputation secretary in 1956 until 1968, when Bill Hopewell was named deputation secretary. Harold continued as candidate secretary until 1980 when he was succeeded by Bill Commons.

After serving as co-director for eight years, Don Trott was appointed executive administrator of enlistment and pre-field ministries in 1995.

Candidate seminar

ENLISTMENT

The enlistment department helps select, screen, train, and send those whom the local church has set apart for missionary service. ABWE provides opportunities for people of all ages to discover missions firsthand. **Expedition** is the program developed by Mark and Nancy Nelson in 1997 for **high school students**. Under the supervision of trained leaders, they experience cross-cultural missions. Through the **IMPACT** program (International Ministry Programs And Cross-cultural Training),

college age and young adults experience living and working on a mission field. **AMP** (the Assistant Missionary Program) enables **adult professionals** to meet needs in areas of targeted temporary ministries.

Expedition team in Arequipa, Peru

PRE-FIELD

In 1982, director Mel Cuthbert coined the term "pre-field ministries" to emphasize a new mindset, with the focus on ministry. The department serves local churches by offering assistance to pastors and their newly appointed missionaries. In 1993, Loren Andersen became director of pre-field ministries.

An IMPACT team member looks on as a Hungarian man reads a tract

Harold Amstutz

Back row: Brian Eichelberger, Henry Lehman, Joe Franz, Paul Sturgis, Bob Auffort, Spencer Jackson, William Pierson, Bob Hammaker, Glenn Priddy, Dave Purrington, Don Davis, Bill Rohweder
Middle row: Nathan Burgess, Bonnie Winey, Dottie Kocher, Nancy Anderson, Jennifer Bufflap, Donna Knight, Julie Grove, Sharon Hammaker, Eunice Priddy, Pam Purrington, Christi Whitcomb, Dick Mitchell, Glenn Barnhart
Seated: Fran Weddle, Vicky Biller, Sara Potter, Gloria Mackey, Joan Damey, John and Louise Williams (volunteers), Jan Ruff, Chloe Mitchell
Not pictured: Neil Glotfelty, Diana and Larry Inskeep, Terry Large, Carol Moser

FINANCE & OPERATIONS DIVISION

This division includes corporate and missionary finance, donor relations, planned giving, information systems, buildings and grounds maintenance, and special projects.

Edward C. Bomm and his wife, Marian, joined ABEO in 1935 and went as missionaries to the Philippines. Ed pastored First Baptist Church in Manila, directed the Manila Evangelistic Institute, and served as the mission's business representative in Manila until the Bomms were imprisoned by the Japanese during World War II.

The Bomms returned to the United States in 1949 and Ed became ABWE's treasurer. He also acted as personnel director and assistant to the president until his retirement in 1971.

Donald Drake joined the staff in 1957 and served for seven years, followed by board member Donald Sutherland. Robert Auffort, an accountant, joined the finance department in 1966. Glenn Priddy came to ABWE in 1995 after years of missionary service with two other organizations. He was made director of missionary finance in 1998.

INFORMATION SYSTEMS

Paul Sturgis developed the IS department in 1986. Part of the department's responsibilities include assessing hardware and software viability, maintaining the computer and telephone equipment, and upgrading the systems. Paul handed over the IS department to Neil Glotfelty in 2001. Neil oversees a network of 125 computers.

SPECIAL PROJECTS

Ralph Gruenberg, an engineer and pastor, was appointed to oversee construction of the Administration and Training Center in Harrisburg. He has also used his skills in Africa, Asia, Europe, and South America to assist in the design and construction of 71 facilities.

In 1967, William Pierson joined ABWE. Today he is the mission treasurer as well as executive administrator of development and finance.

"ABWE is a faith mission and is totally dependent on prayer and the gifts of God's people."
— Lucy Peabody, 1928

Miss Alice Hudson, the second treasurer of ABEO/ABWE, held this honorary post from 1928 to 1947.

Ed and Marian Bomm

Ralph Gruenberg organized the renovation of a church in Kusel, Germany, in 1998.

Back row: Bob Henry, Kristen Stagg, Barney Brumbaugh (volunteer), Wayne Haston, Derek Purrington, Mark Henry
Middle row: Jeff Raymond, Pat Henry, Sharon Haston, Cindy Carmer, Sharon Commons, Jessica Kissell, Ann Washer
Seated: Miranda Yeung, Jeannie and Wally Stephenson, Patti Haller, E. C. Haskell

MISSION RELATIONS DIVISION

This division is the public relations arm of the mission and also oversees the 65 full-time and 13 part-time employees at the International Administration and Training Center. An additional 15 volunteers carry out regular assignments each week.

MEDIA DEPARTMENT

The media department provides support to missionaries by helping create presentations and providing workshops that allow missionaries to produce their own materials.

"Will this picture illustrate to people what we're going to do?"

Carl Brandon, who expanded the communications department

PUBLICATIONS DEPARTMENT

In the fall of 1929, Lucy Peabody put out ABEO's first official publication, which contained, in boldface and large type, these words: "The Apostolic Method and the Apostolic Message through the power of the Holy Spirit will evangelize the world." This slogan created the title for ABWE's official publication, the *Message.* The department also produces books telling what God is doing in missions around the world today.

CHURCH RELATIONS DEPARTMENT

The church relations department communicates through a variety of media to thousands of churches and pastors who support ABWE. Pastors' interfaces, Mobilizing Children to Serve the Lord seminars, and "Vacation With a Purpose" world mission cruises are just a few of the events this department organizes.

E. C. Haskell with pastors at a Pastors' Interface

"Happy Birthday, dear Dick," the ABWE staff sang on September 26, 2001, as Richard Morrison celebrated his 89th birthday. He and his wife, Yvonne, represent volunteers—of all ages—who donate hours of service. His name card says, "I Am Needed." Yes, you are, Richard, as are hundreds more volunteers.

From left: Jim Ruff, Wayne Haston, Carolyn Haskell

CENTER FOR EXCELLENCE IN INTERNATIONAL MINISTRY

In 1997, the Intercultural Training Center was born as the culmination of discussion and prayer concerning a training program for ABWE missionaries. Since the training division would require intense effort and ministry experience, Wendell Kempton appointed veteran missionary and church planter Bob Dyer as the first director of ITC. In 1999, Jim Ruff, church planter and educator from Japan, was named associate director.

Bob developed the ITC program to emphasize hands-on, interactive training. He revamped the pre-field seminar and missionary enrichment conference to include training components and developed in-service training for missionaries.

In 2001 when Bob Dyer returned to church planting, Michael Loftis announced that Dr. Wayne Haston would direct the Center for Excellence in International Ministry, replacing the ITC.

Bob Dyer leads a session on strategic planning.

Dedication of the Training Center, November 2001

Wayne Haston, Tim Blazer, John Peterson

"A missionary who is not growing [professionally], seriously jeopardizes the present and future of his calling and ministry. This neglect radically impacts other members of the ABWE family . . ."

—Dr. Wendell Kempton, Report to the Board, April 1998

More than half a century ago I was invited to join the board of what is now A.B.W.E.

I was drawn to accept due to two issues. First it was at the forefront among independent Baptist missions in standing for the fundamentals of the faith and against the modernism of the time. Second it was committed to evangelism and church planting.

My investment of life through these years in A.B.W.E. has been a source of joy — many days given to Christ and His cause.

Joseph M. Stowell II

Isa 58:10,11
K.J.V.

Dr. Joseph M. Stowell II, ABWE's longest-serving board member, was elected to the advisory council in June 1940 and to the full board and executive committee in 1950. He served as vice president of ABWE from 1955 to 1986.

ABWE BOARDS

In the fall of 2001, the ABWE board met to determine its top 10 priorities as it oversees the ministries of the mission: to insure integrity of the total ministry; develop or approve wise policy; select, support, and evaluate the president; minister to the missionaries; ensure adequate long-term planning; elect, educate, and evaluate the board itself; lead spiritually; ensure adequate resources for the ministry; serve as a problem-resolving resource to the administrators; and publicly promote the ministry of ABWE.

ABWE—CANADA

In the late 1940s, deputation secretary Don Moffat visited London Bible Institute in Ontario to recruit Canadian missionaries. Five couples who responded were appointed under ABWE.

In order to issue tax-deductible receipts to Canadian donors, ABWE formed a corporation comprised mostly of Canadian citizens. David Irwin acted as chairman of the Canadian Council for 25 years, a position now held by Dr. Marvin Brubacher.

Rev. Leander Roblin was appointed as a representative of the mission to churches and schools across Canada in 1961, followed by Rev. Reg and Helen Snell in 1979, and later Ivor and Ruth Greenslade.

In 1975, following the death of his wife Dorothy, Mel Cuthbert returned from Brazil to establish an actual Canadian office. Since 1992, Frank and Brenda Bale, ABWE missionaries in Brazil and Portugal, have served as Canadian director.

> "As the mission launches its ministry into the 21st Century, the ABWE global team, along with our partners in local churches around the world, can be thankful for the cumulative wisdom, experience, and leadership that resides on the ABWE board."
> —Michael Loftis

Canadian Council

"Ramblin' with Am-Blin" (1963), Harold Amstutz and Leander Roblin

ABWE board, September 2001

Schaff Building, Philadelphia

Cherry Hill, New Jersey

Harrisburg, Pennsylvania

ABWE OFFICES

ABWE HEADQUARTERS

The Association of Baptists for Evangelism in the Orient was born in August 1927 on a verandah in Watch Hill, Rhode Island. Early business was conducted from Lucy Peabody's home in Beverly, Massachusetts. In the fall of 1932, the mission's first business office was opened in the Schaff building at 1505 Race Street in Philadelphia. Later, the office relocated to occupy the entire thirteenth floor, employing about 20 people.

In 1970, construction began on 5.6 acres of land along Springdale Road in Cherry Hill, New Jersey. The move from Philadelphia was made in the summer of 1971.

In May 1991, the ABWE board voted to make a major move to Harrisburg, Pennsylvania. The mission purchased 136 acres that included a three-residence complex in New Cumberland, Pennsylvania. With more than 1,000 volunteers from 26 states and six countries, the existing buildings were expanded to meet the mission's ongoing growth.

CANADIAN OFFICE

Cathy Smith (seated), Sharon DePhillippeaux, and Frank Bale in the Canadian office

Rotunda in the Harrisburg office

Securing a support on a snowy day

"And these stones shall be for a memorial forever."

MILESTONES

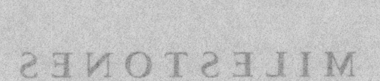

MILESTONES

FROM THE PAST TO THE FUTURE

FAITHFUL UNTO DEATH

During the 75 years ABWE missionaries have proclaimed the gospel, they have enjoyed God's protection during extreme situations, including war, cyclone, and famine. The majority of missionaries lived to retire from the mission field. A significant number, however, contracted diseases or were killed in accidents, many of them while serving on the mission field. The individuals listed here recognized the challenges posed by God's call on their lives, but remained dedicated to the task. We salute them for their sacrificial service in spreading the good news of salvation through Jesus Christ. Countries in parentheses indicate field(s) of service.

Lyn Ambacher
October 27, 1999
(Hong Kong)

Terry Armstrong
June 30, 1992 (Peru,
Colombia, USA)

Roni Bowers
April 20, 2001, in Peru

Terry Bowers
July 6, 1991 (Brazil)

Merle Buckingham
December 22, 1968,
in the Philippines

Chuck Cook
July 3, 1980 (Brazil)

Dorothy Cuthbert
September 17, 1974,
in Brazil

Harold Davis
March 11, 1993,
in Colombia

Gene (DeVries) Ebersole
November 25, 1964
(Philippines)

Rose Durham
September 11, 1971
(Philippines)

Butch Fisher
March 2, 1989,
in Australia

Judy Frerichs
August 2, 1994
(Peru)

Cindy Gelatt
June 12, 1996
(Argentina)

Harry Goehring
June 15, 1965,
in East Pakistan

Herman Harrell
March 11, 1970, while
on pre-field for Brazil

Dorothy Hopper
December 25, 1965,
in the Philippines

Frank Jenista
October 29, 1984,
in Papua New Guinea

Laura Kasten
August 20, 1979
(Philippines)

Eunice Kintner
June 18, 1974,
in the Philippines

Timothy Kunkel
May 6, 1982, while on
pre-field for Peru

Janet Lewis
September 17, 1974,
in Brazil

Sandra Lyons
October 31, 1999
(Peru and Home Office)

Michael and Gladys Martin
January 12, 1980,
while on pre-field for
the Philippines

Tim Matchett
October 24, 1999, in Togo

Carl Matthews
May 18, 1966, in Brazil

Virginia (LeSuer) McClanahan
February 3, 1988 (Brazil)

Paul Miller
May 4, 1959,
in East Pakistan

Effie Olsen
June 26, 1948, in Peru

Harold Palmer
October 20, 1942,
in the Philippines

Tom Pann
October 22, 1980
(Philippines and
Papua New Guinea)

De Elda Payton
November 10, 1995
(Philippines and USA)

Bob Petro
March 7, 2002
in the Philippines

Joan Reid
December 17, 1969,
in Hong Kong

Carol Roduner
March 8, 1979, in Peru

Clarence Russell
fall 1952, while on pre-field
for the Philippines

David Savage
September 13, 1995,
while on pre-field for Peru

Vada Shook
March 23, 1988 (Japan)

Louise Stephenson
May 22, 1993, while on
pre-field for South Africa

Grace Stull
October 5, 1979,
in Brazil

Dave Taylor
December 9, 1998,
in Brazil

Bev Toro
March 16, 1992
(Chile, Australia, USA)

Lori VanEtten
August 25, 1988, while on
pre-field for USA

Kathy Vidal
November 23, 1983 (USA)

Dal Washer
May 25, 1989, in Togo

David Wilkinson
January 25, 1993,
in Papua New Guinea

Marie Wisner
December 12, 1962
(Brazil)

Jan Wolfe
August 13, 1982
(Bangladesh)

"Be thou faithful unto death, and I will give thee a crown of life."
—Revelation 2:10

DALLAS WASHER
"BELOVED HUSBAND AND FATHER"
DECEMBER 29, 1921 - MAY 25, 1989
"PASTEUR TSITSI"
PIONNIER de la MISSION ABWE au TOGO

"I HAVE BUT ONE CANDLE OF LIFE TO BURN
AND WOULD RATHER BURN IT OUT
WHERE PEOPLE ARE DYING IN DARKNESS
THAN IN A LAND WHICH IS FLOODED WITH LIGHTS"

Willard Stull; Dan and Diana (Stull) Richner; Randy and Cindy (Commons) Richner, Ariana and Joel

David and Evelyn Southwell; Randy and Sarah Southwell, Victoria, Elaina, and Lucas; Christie (Southwell) and Mike Wilkerson, Taylor and Bryce

MKs have more fun than a barrel of monkeys.

Third generation missionaries who are part of the ABWE family:

Russ Ebersole IV (Togo): parents, Russ and Gene Ebersole (Philippines); grandparents, Henry and Gladys DeVries (Philippines)

Randy Richner (Brazil): parents, Dan and Diana Richner (Brazil); grandparents, Willard and Grace Stull (Brazil)

Cindy Richner (Brazil): parents, Bill and Sharon Commons (Hong Kong); grandparents, Harold and Corinth Commons (ABWE president, 1935–1971)

Carol Scruggs (Brazil): parents, Dick and Joyce Matthews (Brazil); grandparents, Carleton and Mary Adelaide Matthews (Brazil)

David Southwell (Brazil): parents, Dave and Evelyn Southwell (Brazil and Portugal); grandparents, Don and Helen Hare (Brazil)

Randy Southwell (Brazil): parents, Dave and Evelyn Southwell (Brazil and Portugal); grandparents, Don and Helen Hare (Brazil)

"One generation shall praise thy works to another, and shall declare thy mighty acts."

—Psalm 145:4

Currently 69 missionary kids (MKs) have been appointed to career missionary service. Of that number, 49 returned to the country where their parents served (or still serve, in some cases). Another 28 missionaries' parents served with other mission boards.

SENDING CHURCHES

From its inception, ABWE placed the highest priority on its relationships with local churches. These partnerships enable ABWE to expedite the churches' mandate to reach the nations of the world. Among the churches which supported ABEO in its early days as a mission were **Chelsea Baptist**, Atlantic City, New Jersey; **Calvary Baptist**, New York City; **First Baptist**, Atlantic City, New Jersey; **First Baptist**, Hackensack, New Jersey; **Garfield Baptist**, Milwaukee, Wisconsin; **Tabernacle Baptist**, Seattle, Washington; **Walnut Street Baptist**, Waterloo, Iowa; and **Wealthy Street Baptist**, Grand Rapids, Michigan.

In 1934, the General Association of Regular Baptist Churches (GARBC) voted officially to endorse ABEO. That same year, **Haddon Heights Baptist Church** in New Jersey hosted ABEO's annual meeting, the beginning of many years of faithful financial support and supplying personnel for the mission.

A new vehicle given to missionaries by a supporting church

Jay Walsh (second from right), with Lakefield's young people in front of the original church building

A MISSION CHURCH GROWS ABWE MISSIONARIES

Home missionaries who started Lakefield Baptist Church in Michigan's Upper Peninsula grew a whole crop of ABWE missionaries. When the first foreign missionary spoke in that little church in 1949, Jay Walsh and Eleanor Reed (the pastor's daughter) responded to his challenge to give their lives to serve anywhere in the world, should God so lead. They married and served in Bangladesh for 35 years. A couple of years later, Shirley Harkness responded to God's call and served for 24 years as an MK teacher in Bangladesh. Later still, Ruth Teed yielded her life to the Lord. She married Frank Finch, and they served the Lord for 14 years in the Philippines.

British philosopher

Edmund Burke once said, "You can never plan the future by the past." The apostle Paul, veteran missionary, put it another way, "Brethren, I count not myself to have apprehended: but this one thing I do, forgetting those things which are behind, and reaching forth unto those things which are before, I press toward the mark for the prize of the high calling of God in Christ Jesus" (Philippians 3:13–14).

Missionaries are always on a journey, always cutting new roads, leaving new milestones, always moving forward. Reviewing this book has been a wonderful rest by the wayside, but now it is time to pick up the bags and consider the future. We can do that knowing we will have plenty of "time" in eternity to visit around the campfires

*"Therefore, since we have so great a cloud of witnesses surrounding us . . .
let us run with endurance the race that is set before us, fixing our eyes
on Jesus, the author and perfector of faith."*

—Hebrews 12:1–2

of heaven and review the glorious victories and stops along our earthly journey.

Where will the milestones of the future be placed? At some bend in the road, at some crossroad of decision, in some quiet glen where a co-worker rests in peace? Whether or not the milestones we place will be considered significant is not ours to decide. Those who follow us—and eventually our Lord Himself—will decide.

And where are we headed to now? To multiply ourselves around the world. To make disciples, to plant churches, to mentor missionaries who will be sent from every nation to every people on earth. Imagine the milestones they will leave on the unmapped paths of the world. Heaven must have a room where we will be able to view the milestones of missions.

—Michael G. Loftis,
President

ABEO and ABWE Missionaries by Candidate Class

Listed below are all missionaries appointed by the board of ABWE, regardless of their ultimate arrival or number of terms of service on any ABWE field. Please note that many individuals who have worked in sensitive areas are not named here for security reasons.

ABEO

1929

R. C. and Norma Thomas
Ellen Martien
Paul and Margaret Culley
Lillian Culley
Bessie Traber
Alice Drake
Helen Hinkley
Percy Pamberton
Mr. and Mrs. M. W. Castrodale

1930

Bernice Hahn
Edith Webster
Ellis and Ruth Skolfield
Edna Hotchkiss
Alexander Sutherland

1932

Mr. and Mrs. Russell Jones
Bethel France
Stella Mower

1934

Esther Yerger
Ruth Woodworth

1935

Evelyn Congleton
Mrs. John B. Champion
Ed and Marian Bomm

1936

Eleanor Bailey
Beulah Heaton
Thomas Taggart
Norm and Florence MacPherson
Bernard Bancroft
Sadie Busse
Ruth Grimshaw
Charles Entner
Francis Hirschy (engaged to C. Entner)

1937

Robert Smallwood
F. W. and Maretia Naylor
Samuel Fisk

1938

William Webster
Henry and Gladys DeVries
Robert and Grace Kohler
James and Edna Ker
Elizabeth Hiestand
Elsie Parks

1939

Paul and Kay Friederichsen

ABWE BEGINS

William and Elva Scherer
Mona Kemery
Rhoda Little

1940

William and Ethel Goldie
Harold and Esther Palmer
Louise Lynip

Earl and Rachel Roberts
Elsie Howell
James and Anna Ryan

1941

Robert and Mildred Arthur

1942

Donald and Edna Davis
Robert and Bertha Standley
Robert and Francis Burns

1943

James and Helen Carder
Harry and Wilma Stahlman
Orville and Helen Floden

1944

Donald and Helen Hare
Dorothy Palmer
Virginia LeSuer
Carleton and Mary Adelaide Matthews

1945

Victor and Margaret Barnett
Jeanne Wagner
Edwin and Helen Spahr
Helen Paige

1946

Jay and Dorothy Morgan
Hettie Todd
Gordon and Martha Wray
Edna Hull
Dorothy LeViness
Blakely and Sylvania Rogers
Ernest and Effie Olsen

1947

Edith Smith
William McCarty

Paul and Helen Miller
Kathryn Klitch
Daniel and Lauretta Holden
Walter and Ellen Craymer
William and Ruth Hopewell
Robert Banning
Elaine Snyder (engaged to R. Banning)
Gerald Rose
Walter and Lillian Binney
Lincoln and Lenore Nelson
Campbell and Lois Murdoch

1948

Donald and Kay Rogers
William and Dorothy Hopper
Alfred and Ruth Conant
John and Marion Loggans
Cleveland and Helen McDonald
Kenneth and Jean Mitchell
Frank and Sophie Jenista
Louella Loewen
Hedwig Helsten

1949

Alma Shoemaker
Royer and Hazel Allman
Humbert and Jeanne Tentarelli
Oral and Eunice Kintner
Thomas and Alice Secore
Nevin and Dorothy Beehler
Frona Mattox
Jerome and Dorothy Casner
William and Ruth Large
Jack and Joyce Looney
Ruth Stewart
Robert and Jean Farra
Bonnie Guthrie
Laureda Thompson
David and Maver Hiebert
Frank and Doris Jertberg

1950

Harry and Winnifred Allum
Warren and Mary West
Eugene and Earlene Wellsfry
Douglas and Virginia Saxby
Stanley and Jean Holman
George and Lillian Toensfeldt
Paul and Jessie Schlener
John and Fran Schlener
Mildred Crouch
Priscilla Bailey
Virginia Martin
Helen Bailey

1951

Arthur and Joyce Cavey
Ronald and Laura Esson
Jean Ferguson
Ellen Morgan
Marion Schwenk
Helen Smith
Lindsey and Jean Harrell
Laura Kasten
Harold and Lois Ruth Chilton
Clarence and Mary Russell

1952

Harold and Althea Tooley
Vernon and Marian Chandler
Elaine Potter
Donald and Pauline Taber
Catherine Mollohan
Margaret Bock
Harry and Vickie Buerer
Melbourne and Dorothy Cuthbert

1953

Carrel and Fern Aagard
Carson Fremont
William and Joan Reid
Dortha Warner

Ruth Warner
Arthur and Harriette Christmann
Jay and Norma Dyksterhouse
Russell and Gene Ebersole
Doris Secor
Winifred Morrette
Mary O'Neill
Robert Nutt
Richard and Rose Durham
Paul and Vada Shook
Nathaniel and Esther Mitchell
Orlan and Mabel Wilhite
Elmer and Marjorie Cassidy

1954

Henry and Virginia DeVries (Jr.)
Earl and Phyllis Carlberg
John and Catherine Kennedy
Ivor and Ruth Greenslade
Donald and Mary Lee Lang
Virginia Forkell
Jeanne Marion
Mary Goodson
Charles and Ruth Mitchell
Joyce Hatch
Richard and Ruth Gray
Mr. and Mrs. Joseph Kegans
Ralph and Joanna Vile
Virginia Allen
Jacque and Drusilla Schultz
Norman and Margaret Gentry
Frank and Jean Morse
Clinton and Dorothy Bonnell
Rosemary Ullery
Bessie Turnbull
Gladys MacLean
Walter and Melba Nicholls

1955

Fred McClanahan
Victor and Margaret Barnard

Donald and Vivian Bond
Cathleen Kendall
Starling Post
Mabel Post
Ronald and Gladys Mezner
Robert and Corinth Wanstall
Harold and Vivienne House
Merle and Joyce Buckingham
George and Marie Wisner
Ivan and Daphne Lee

1956

Ralph and Marjorie Poulson
Gerald Russell
Richard and Betty Sterkenberg
Eugene and Elizabeth Gurganus
Richard Tice
David and Beulah Sheridan
Ella Grover
George and Norma Haberer
Corris Carlson
Dale and Martha Payne
Juanita Canfield
Mary Lou Brownell

1957

Miriam Morin
Joyce Ann Wingo
Thelma James
Blanche Hamilton
Gerald and Virginia Winters
John and Pearl Sarjeant
William and Rosalind Stoner
Charles and Caroline Porter

1958

Robert and Caroline Anthony
Darline Fremont
Edward and Dorothy Blakslee
Glen and Jean Hunt
Charles Runyon

Henry and Ruth Scheltema
James and Elma Turek
D. Jay and Eleanor Walsh

1959

Donna Alhgrim
Lawrence and Jacqueline Armstrong
David and Joan Gardner
Henry and Arla Lee Hoffman
Leland and Jo Ann Lanier
Raymond and Janet Lewis
Viggo and Joan Olsen
Peter and Vivian Skogerbo
David and Beverly Toro
Francais Weddle

1960

Bonnie Abbas
Helen Aguilar
William and Thespena Branda
Evelyn Morgan
Frederic and Rachel Patton
Benjamin and Pauline Peterson
Lynn Silvernale
Willard and Grace Stull
Horace and Doris Williams

1961

Ralph and Lucille Ankenman
Melvin and Marjorie Beals
Rebecca Davey
Glenda Geiszler
Harry and Nancy Goehring
Donn and Pauline Ketcham
Jeannie Lockerbie
Richard and Joyce Matthews
Duane Roduner
Jean Weld

1962

Robert and Barbara Adolph
Harry and Lyn Ambacher
Robert and Grace Beikert
Terrance and Wilma Bowers
Chuck and Adelaide Cook
Lois Cooper
Richmond and Dolores Donaldson
James and Sharon Evans
Diane Foote
Gustav and Sharon Kasten
Sandra Lyons
Reid Minich
Richard and Marion Morey
Robert and Margaret Paswaters
Carol Roduner
Raydene Taylor
Betty Whitenack

1963

Dorothy Bornschlegel
Larry and Jane Golin
Agnes Haik
Robert and Esther Howder
Harold and Janice Jefferis
Robert and Minnie Jobe
DeElda and Nancy Payton

1964

Mildred Cooley
Jesse and Joyce Eaton
Norman and Bobbie Fay
Marilyn Malmstrom
Sheldon and Cora Lee Peck
John and Jean Peterson
Larry and Beverly Smith
Florence Theaker
Doris Ward

1965

Flay and Margaret Allen
William and Sharon Commons
Nancy Crosser
Frank and Nancy Hartwig
John Kallin
Jean Shawver
Donald and Ruth Trott
Lois Wantoch

1966

Bruce and Marlene Anderson
Willard Benedict
Larry and Marilyn Boehning
Richard and Mavis Buck
Sylvia Cline
Charles and Judy Frerichs
Shirley Harkness
Robert and Pat Henry
Janet Oursler
Robert and Karen Shumaker
Robert and Lynne Trout
Leigh and Charlotte Upchurch
Paul and Judy Van Kleek
Robert and Rita Wright
William and Cathryn Wuth

1967

James and Sheilia Ankney
James and Esther Entner
Robert and Sandra Hedrick
Norman and Evelyn Nicklas
Gary and Wilma Sammons
Daniel and Judith Smith
William Stevenson
Gretchen Talen
Sandra Thompson

1968

Jack and Margaret Archibald
David and Charlotte Boehning
Richard and Daneth Brown
Donald and Janice Fanning
Gwendolyn Geens
William and Patsy Hawk
Darlene Hull
Joseph Massey
Linda Short
Gale and Sharron Smith

1969

Susan Breckley
Merry Davey
Joseph and Joyce DeCook
Shirley Dick
Robert and Lois Dyer
David and Darlene Fidler
Herman and Charlene Harrell
Neil and Sandra Heim
Mary Massey
Ronald and Cheryl Perrine
Sharon Row
Shelby Spradlin
David and Barbara Taylor
Muriel Waite
George Weber
Janice Wolfe

1970

Marilyn Arrowood
Frank and Brenda Bale
Patricia Barkley
Teresa Boice
Lyle and Patricia Culberson
Richard and Marcia Ernst
Roger and Joyce Fenton
Robert and Linda Franklin
Butch and Bonnie Jarvis
Robert and Sandra Phillips
John Powers
Marilyn Stevenson
Nancy Towle
Philip and Ruth Young

1971

David and Susan Blazer
Dwayne Buker
Donald and Barbara Bromley
Kathleen Cartner
Daniel and Maryanna Horton
Melvin and Julia Lacock
Donald and Barbara Love
Edward and Marjorie Pierce
Leon and Patricia Small
William and Etta Stevenson
Larry and Rose Anne Thornburg
David and Doris Totman

1972

John and Vira Baker
David and Susan Black
Roxanne Brodeur
Rachel Buker
John and Hortense Bullock
Mark and Janice Chandler
Sally Gott
Garry and Ann McInnis
Debra Mitchell
Paul and Judy Muzzey
Dennis and Ruth Oatley
Alice Payne
Larry Secrest
Richard and Carol Stagg
Terry and Carole Tufts
Jack and Karen Willsey

1973

Dorothy Adams
Carol Bibighaus
Karen Carder
Carol Ciocca
Richard and Jo Ann Davis
David and Elwanda Fields
Gordon and Bess Finley
Larry and Thelma Holman

Thomas and Penny Latham
Dora Marxman
Michael and Elaine McCubbins
Tim and Esther Neufeld
Larry and Jane Parks
James and Carole Plunkitt
Mary Lou Powers
David and Evelyn Southwell
Dallas and Kay Washer
Ronald and Kathleen Weber
Robyn Westbrook

1974

Cameron and Grace Bacon
Norman and Louise Barnard
Gerald and Linda Etheridge
Susanne Farley
Margaret Garrett
Violet Hart
Dallas and Kay Hyatt
Craig and Elaine Kennedy
Andrew and Diane Large
Thomas and Elizabeth Peace
Harry and Ann Rogers
Bonnie Secrest
Carolynn Sharp
David Sizemore
John and Roberta Stevenson
Joan Voss
Duane and Dianne Waterland
Gerald Williams
Michael and Sharon Williams

1975

Richard and Libby Basler
David and Pamela Bennett
Samuel and Demaris Bolet
Charles and Nancy Burkett
John Check
Randall and Phyllis Cook
Barbara Cooper

Cynthia DeBrosse
Nancie Dellaganna
Kathleen Hopkins
Timothy and Jane Kunkel
Robert and Serena Myers
David and Rebecca Nelson
Sonia Nelson
Samuel and Judith Olsen
Edith Phillips
Gloria Reid
Joyce Rudduck
James and Janet Ruff
Ernest and Wilma Traeger
Steve and Julia Trescott
Robert and Lois Walsh
Ronald and Ann Washer
Sandra Weigle
Bob and Doris Wigden
Daniel Winters

1976

Alice Augsburger
Bernard and Carole Beverly
Kenneth Cole
Paul and Patricia Collier
Harold and Melody Davis
Clarence and Dora Fisher
Dale and Beverly Fogg
Richard and Patricia Glenny
Elizabeth Gunther
Lois Habrial
Gail Hopkins
Jeanne Jensma
Roy Jones
Carol McCaffery
Thomas and Kathleen Pann, Sr.
Ila Pechumer
Charles and Janet Robinson
Larry and Sandra Rowland
Jewl Ann Spoelhof
Glenn and Beverly Stewart

Mary Ann Thompson
Dennis and Diane Washer
Janice Whetstone
Annette Williams

1977

Larry and Nancy Allen
Carol Baldwin
John and Lolita Barram
Darrell and Sandra Blankenship
Neville Chin
Judith Fabisch
Paul and Marla Fields
Sue Hahn
Clifton and Hannah Jensen
Philip Klumpp
Paul and Jill Moser
Mallory and Judy Parmerlee
Yvonne Shuttleworth
William and Susan Spoelhof
Donald Thompson
Roberta Wills
Lee and Sharon Wise

1978

Nancy Andersen
John Baab
Mark and Debra Ann Baker
Stephen and Karen Borders
Steven and Jo Ann Carter
David and Kathleen Clutts
Richard and Ila Coleman
Allan and Robin Cuthbert
George and Joyce Goodwin
Jon and Kathy Griffin
Quentin and Claudia Haase
Bill and Patricia Hawley
Thomas and Susan Jertberg
Clarence and Peggy Ledford
Michael and Gladys Martin
George and Eleanor McCullagh

Bruce and Beverly McDonald
Richard and Anna Merkel
Robert and Jimmie Nusca
Mel and Ruby Pittman
Dan and Charlene Rider
Sally Sayger
Ronald and Christine Self
Kenneth and Renny Snare
Jack and Sandra Sorg
David and Evelyn Stone
Wayne and Dorothy Tabberer
Christine Thompson
Sue Thomson
James and Ruth Turpin

1979

Goldie Anderson
Stephen and Martha Anderson
Christine Beal
David and Vicki Jo Bennett
Michael Chiano, Jr.
David and Cherri Cooper
Melvin and Patricia Cummings
Roger and Lynda Curtis
Gilbert and Marilyn Dickinson
Michael and Kathryn Glazier
James and Denise Greenacre
Stacie Gump
Paul and Suzie Hardy
Jerry and Cynthia Harris
Jerry and Donna Layton
Kenneth and Barnetta Lesta
David and Karen Long
Gary and Deborah Manter
Timothy and Helen Matchett
Sheryl Mixon
Beverly Quinney
Daniel and Shelley Reichard
Vera Roduner
Don and Dora Taylor
Lee and Barbara Thompson

1979 continued

Peggy Williams

Joyce Wilson

1980

Rebecca Allen

Susan Arnold

Frederick and Tracy Barlow

Marc and Judie Blackwell

Johnny and Susan Bolin

Daniel and Teresa Cecil

James and Gail Christian

Robert and Shirley Cropsey

Ann Den Uyl

Richard and Joy Dietrich

William and Melody Dooley

Douglas and Sharon Fry

Charles and Gloria Garringer

Robert and Janice Goddard

Marla Groh

Eloise Haven

Paul and Kathy Holritz

Marilyn Horne

Gene and Judy King

John and Cynthia Koster

Dale and Karen Marshfield

George and Carolyn Martens

Rebecca McGregor

Barbara Nelson

Jerold and Lynda Neuman

David and Peggy Pardini

Andrew and Karen Rice

David and Ruth Rogers

Vicki Shaw

Steven and Judy Shook

Jack and Marilyn Slough

Charles and Elsie Smith

Roger and Marcy Smith

Jerry and Mary Jo Troyer

Terry and Sandra Washer

Floyd and Lois Wilcox

Allen and Kimberly Yoder

1981

Mary Lou Berghuis

Rodney and Kathy Churchill

George and Debra Collins

Mark Henzler

Stephen and Kris Holman

Dorothy Kroeger

Laura Kuykendall

James and Allene Latzko

James and Pam Leffew

Philip and Kitty McMillen

Bonnie O'Connor

Robert and Barbara Quick

Mark and Debbie Richardson

Daniel and Diana Richner

Wayne and Sue Robertson

Jack and Cheryl Shiflett

David and Wendy Stoner

Timothy and Lorna Lee Tucker

Mark and Marian Willey

Ruth Yocom

1982

Randy and Jeanette Alderman

Edward and Marla Allston

Keith and Mary Anderson

Samuel and Audrey Carr

Michael and Debbie Edwards

Samuel and Darlene Farlow

Thomas and Nancy Farlow

Michael and Vicky Fester

Daniel and Cynthia Gelatt

Ted and Mary Sue Hall

Richard and Angela Hurd

Don and Lisa Jennings

William and Linda McNiece

Larry and Heather Nutbrown

Sharon Payne

Lynn Retzer

Jonathan and Marilyn Rust

Ronald and Pamela Smith

Arlie and Debra Spargur

Russell Stockman

Barbara Stubbeman

Rodney and Angela Stucky

David and Lori VanEtten

Linda VanMeter

Ann Wahlgren

Karen Wales

James and Janet Ward

Thomas and Lela Wilhite

1983

Walter and Lois Anderson

David and Anita Devore

Kevin and Bobbi Donaldson

Steve and Debi Douglas

Sally Finck

Larry and Caroline Hultquist

Laura Lehto

Jim and Marilou Long

Howard and Virginia McClure

Melissa McWilliams

John and Michele Morgan

David and Virginia Morris

Steve and Joan Mortimer

Carol Moser

Lynn Porter

Karen Seymour

Sherry Skirrow

Joann Smith

Grace Stoddart

Grady and Cindy Toland

Mark and Judy Wood

Ruth Wood

1984

Mark and Terri Bagwell

Bill and Barbara Barrick

Glenn and Dorothy Budd

Pat Duell

Frank and Ruth Finch

Mike Fite

Richard and Ruth Gelina

Shawne Gelina

Mark and Andrea Gregory

Jan Helsel

Ken and Sue James

George and Karen King

David and Julie Rudolph

Lynn Ruffner

Jane Schmitz

Paul and Sandra Schultz

Carl Sexton

Teresa Stenoien

Gil and Denise Thomas

Bill and Debbie Tobias

Tim and Marsha Weeks

Mike and Judy Young

Dave and Patty Zemmer

1985

Sarah Blazer

Gretchen Carter

Cal and Carol Clark

Kent and Kelly Craig

Jack and Kitty Cribbs

Connie Farrington

Wayne and Gail Gasser

Kathy Hadley

Mark and Carol Henry

Gary and Paulette Hill

Arthur and Donna Keaton

Craig and Darlene Kordic

Lucille LeChasseur

Paul and Sharon Leslie

Mel and Shirley Lyons
Steve and Caroline Mann
Steve and Mary Jo Mills
Debbie Newsome
Linhthong and Douangsone Phrasavath
Wayne and Noeline Robilliard
Barney and Adelia Robison
Pete and Penny Sherwood
Robert and Deborah Thompson
Jay and Susan Tilley
Dennis and Amy Toll
John and Geraldine Weeks
James and Carol West
Linda Wood

1986

Joseph and Meta Arthur
Dick and Linda Basler
Dennis and Cathy Callaway
Betsy Coffman
Richmond and Beth Donaldson
Harold and Shawne Ebersole
Susan Edge
Rose Garcia
Paul and Carol Harris
Janice Jefferis
Brian and Carol Kistler
Steven and Kathleen Leeper
Marjorie Lund
William and Nancy Moore
Otto and Lori Reitnauer
Marilyn Scraver
Lois Sexton
Edward and Rebecca Shover
Gary and Corene Spence
William and Karen TenHaaf
Frank and Alves Weirman
Brian Williams

1987

John and Laura Bailey
Jack and Patty Boyer
Chad and Lynette Brosius
Rich and Cindy Brown
Terry and Wendy Broyles
David and Nancy Cropsey
Scott and Robin Dewitt
Bill and Deborah Finch
Dorothy Glorn
Jim and Tanya Goldsmith
Kathy Greenslade
Tonya Harshman
Chris and Lori High
Marvin and Ruth Humphreys
Marcia Kingsbury
Beth Kuhar
Stephen and Becky Little
Robbie and Wanda Locke
Susan Noll
Bill and Becky Petite
Ken and Julia Pollock
Sidney and Janalyce Reed
David and Susan Schmidt
Suzanne Spaulding
David and Dawn Spink
David and Rosezell Stevenson
Linda Telfer
Carole Thayer
Thomas and Kristi Vandenberg
David and Rhonda Wilkinson
Brian and Karen Williams
Faith Williams
Jessica Williams

1988

Robert and Lori Bartram
Greg and Beth Baum
Tim and Diane Bilbrey
Judy Bowen

Peter and Lisa Brock
Merrill and Marsha Corbitt
Bryant and Sharan Crane
Duane and Linda Cross
Brian and Laurel Dix
Donald and Connie Duty
Jerry and Gloria Foster
Rick and Annie Grahame
Jane Hankin
Jackie Hemmings
Timothy and Nancy Hepworth
Mary Israel
Michael and Jo Beth Loftis
Sam and Karen Logan
Brenda Mastin
Alan and Tara Mayhak
Lisa McClure
Keith and Doris McCrory
Brian and Dianna Nester
John Pagan
Don and Gypsy Paulson
Robert and Valerie Petro
Christopher and Elizabeth Prezorski
Thomas Sartor
Bill and Lori Smith
Jim and Lori Spoto
David and Debby Trimbur
Marty and Linda Vidal
Duane and Natalie Wilkins
David and Debbie Woodard

1989

Mary Beth Banning
David and Virginia Boone
Terri Brill
Harry and Janice Gebert
Sandra Green
Richard and Linda Grover
Terence and Christina Havens
Mark and Diane Henzler
Timothy and Joann Hoganson

Kevin and Valerie Johnson
John Lennon
Douglas and Phyllis Morris
Bob and Becky Patten
Rene Ruscella
Scott and Nikki Russell
Jon and Pam Sharp
John and Betty Teusink
Miriam Tyers
David and Nancy Walter
Robert and Kathryn Wilcox

1990

Steve and Sandy Aholt
Shirley Anderson
Russell and Krista Baun
Scott and Lisa Carter
Stephen and Daneene Cottle
Matt and Barbara Douglas
Joan Eaton
Mike and Diane Eleveld
Laura Fouser
Ron and Deretha Garrett
Jennifer Gentzler
Stan and Debbie Haegert
Rocky and Arlene Hartung
Doug and Sharon Kreeger
Rhonda Lennon
David and Jill MacFadden
Pat and Kellis Melson
Tim and Lisa Mundinger
Mark and Susan Nikitin
Dennis and Jan Rost
John and Laurie Russell
Christopher and Donna Sadowitz
Annette Shiley
Lynell Smith
Karen Stagg
John and Aimee Stiles

APPENDIX A

1990 continued

Don Taber
Miriam Wheeler
Alan and Regina Wilson
Tom and Kari Zentz

1991

David and Diane Blackledge
Rob and Kristi Cady
Tom and Paula Carr
Dan and Kelly Cook
Dan and Betsy Delavan
Carol Durey
Bob and Diana Ericsson
Don and Dana Fultz
Tim and Becki Konuch
Gary and Becky Kuhn
Larry and Mary Lowery
Alan and Amy Moody
Luis and Barbara Perez
Bob and Debbie Purnell
Ron and Joanne Reamer
John and Jacky Taylor
Ernie and Lynn Wagner
Dennis and Rachel Weaver
Tim and Sharon Wheeler
David and Julie Zentz

1992

Dan and Debbie Branda
Cindy Carmer
Leon and Donna Duell
Cheryl Dyck
Rick and Carol Ferrari
Bryan and Kim Gregory
Timothy and Winsome Haithcox
Chris and Margaret Hall
Chris and Maylin Hartwick
Bobby and Sara Hile
Chris and Debbie Johnson
Jim and Carla Junge

Jim and Carol King
Nancy LaBonte
Mary LeCouteur
Cami McGraw
Tim and Alice Moody
Wally and Louise Stephenson
Steve and Julie Thompson
Phil and Becky Walsh
Barry and Katherine White
Bob and Lee Ann Wiernusz
Steve and Cheryl Winget

1993

Deb Barnum
Paul Beliasov
Jim and Roni Bowers
Mark and Debbie Christopher
Jean Fote
David and Karen Hamrick
Shawn and Tina Haynie
Emmett and Terron Koch
Robert and Debby Lugar
Jim and Diane Lytle
Donna Messenger
Kevin and Cynthia Reilly
Ruth Rust
David and Lynne Savage
Laurel Sorber
Steve and Etta Stadtmiller
Geoff and Beth Williams

1994

David and Anita Alcorn
Donald and Andrea Allard
Natalie Beck
Nathan and Christine Carmichael
Duane and Katherine Carmody
Timothy and Kiperly Coley
Donald and Cherry Eade
Edward Foster
Steven and Kelley Frerichs

Timothy and Rebekah Gainey
Larry and Sharon Haag
Jonathan and Lori Haskell
David and Billie Holmes
Kurt and Connie Holst
Henry and Janet Houk
Mona Kach
Deborah Lynne Kitchen
David and Joan Knaus
Wendy Kreger
Michael and Liselotte Landoll
Suzanne Lodico
Kenneth and Amy Lowe
Douglas and Sharon Martin
Paul and Diane Osborn
John and Ruth Patton
Gordon and Laurie Phillips
Rebekah Poteat
Randall and Cynthia Richner
Kent and Rebecca Sager
Joan Schmitz
Earl and Marilyn Shaffer
David and Rebecca Staab
Scotte and Elizabeth Ann Staab
Wendy Stiles
David and Penny Winget

1995

Marc Blackwell, Jr.
Michael and June Bradley
Lori Brock
Ronald and Riki Davis
Duane and Susan Early
Robert and Joyce Fry
Kenneth and Ellen Fuss
Daniel and Cynthia Hopkins
Bradley and Elizabeth Howe
Joel and Brenda Jefferis
Terry and Kathleen Jordan
James and April Kane
Stephen and Stephanie Kelly

Audrey Lawrence
Stephen and Susan Mayo
David and Patty McIntyre
Stephen and Kara Murphy
Andrew and Stephanie Pace
Sandra Pratt
Glenn and Eunice Priddy
Franklin and Tamara Roe
Mary Jane Rust
Dianne Sands
Stephen and Carol Scruggs
Joanne Tompkins
Stephen and Janice Trostle
David and Wendy Weaver
Sherry Williams

1996

Stephen and Jill Adolph
Robert and Christine Archibald
Bruce and Carol Bagley
Ronald and Brenda Barnes
David and Teri Buckalew
Catherine Butler
Donald and Gail Craft
James and Joanne Davis
Shelah Dull
Marsha Dunlap
Timothy and Virgie Farley
Jean Frerichs
Joel and Norma Fritch
Jerry and Susan Hamann
Robert and Karen Hamilton
Robert and Rhinda Hayden
Kurt and Barbara Mathews
Kenneth and Julia Morgan
Luke and MaryBeth Puckett
Steven and Terri Robinson
Brian and Crystal Salsman
David and Shawn Smith
Gary and Cynthia Spengler
Mark and Donna Thompson

Michael and Sharon Thompson
Douglas and Kathy Treu
Timothy and Barbara Vermilyea
Douglas and Linda Wilson

1997

Angela Atwell
Jeff and Wendy Beverly
Mark and Jill Billington
Benjamin Chisolm
Patrick and Tina Curby
Randall and Deborah Fish
Heather Fowler
Ed and Carmen Glodfelter
Carolee Graf
Peni Howder
Cynthia McFarland
Antonio and Diana Jo Navarrete
Jerry and Charlotte Patrick
Douglas and Karen Phillips
Christian and Maura Pilet
Kimberly Rae Rosenau
LaMar and Joanna Salley
Randy and Sarah Southwell
Michael and Joan Swanson
Herman and Tami Teachout
Jonathan and Jennifer Trott
Max and Nola Tucker
Calvin Veith
Harvey and Yvonne Wait
Harry and Beatrice Ward
Ted and Diane Weinberg
Thomas and Melinda Williams
Peter and Sonya Wright
Kerry and Wanda Yankowy

1998

Brian and Debbie Beverly
David and Loralee Beverly
Timothy and Andrea Blazer
Patrick and Gina Cassidy

William and Renee Crowe
Greg and Sherry Davidson
Vladimir and Mimoza Dervishi
Jim and Natalie Eaton
Russell and Melody Ebersole
Christy Glover
Nicole Grizenko
Michelle Hammaker
Miriam Hayes
John and Cindy Heath
Beth Isbell
Aaron and Deborah Karr
Don and Nancy Loose
Richard and Chloe Mitchell
Erin Nelson
Ruthanne Raiche
Stephen and Gretchen Root
Mike and Mary Lou Rummey
David and Valerie Smallman
David and Catherine Smith
Norman and Susan Smith
Raymond and Lori Smith
Richard and Carol Stowell
Gary and Mary Jane Strange
Bjorn and Lisa Thomsen
Paul and Laurel Timblin
Stephen and Lourdinha Veness
Paul and Rachel Weber
David and Jodi Wilson
Tom and Nancy Wolf
David and Melanie Woodard
Liza Zamar
David and Janice Zimmer

1999

Tim and Jane Bahula
Emery and Dikola Bragg
Robert and MaryScott Burns
Glenn and Tammy Clodgo
Bradley Collins
Matthew and Amanda Cropsey

Robert Cupps
Jeffrey and Jodi Demerly
Kraig and Anne Elliott
Timothy and Martia Franklin
Rachel Freese
Lisa Giesler
Howard and Linda Hardy
Paul and Penny Hesman
Keith and Jody Hudak
Barry and Linda Jones
Julie McFadden
Timothy and Charlene Miskimen
Ashley Ostman
Calvin and Joyce Voelker
Adrian and Elaine Whitlock

2000

Alejandro and Robyn Armijo
Joshua and Heidi Ausfahl
Melissa Baccarella
Kirk and Annette Barger
Ed and Dana Berry
Suellen Black
Peter and Dawn Bonner
Rebecca Courliss
Patricia Dye
Jim and Kristina Foster
Darlene Gabler
Tammy Gordon
Russell and Mary Huff
Shayam and Paula Khatri
Shane and Erin Latham
Peter and Bibiana Morgan
Lloyd and Athena Peace
Frank and Marlea Pfeiffer
Kent and Sandra Pool
Sharon Rahilly
David and Dennise Rhoads
Buddy and April Robinson
David and Sharon Ronan
Wayne and Susan Royce

Jeffrey and Julie Sanders
Thomas and Susan Scriven
Dennis and Bonnie Slothower
Stephen and Marla Smith
Jerry and Sue Ann Thomas
Olivia Walsh
Rebecca Wine

2001

Judy Andre
Randy and Deborah Austin
Carlton and Karen Baer
Paul and Karolyn Beltz
Jim and Karen Blumenstock
Elisabeth Bowman
Jeffrey and Kristine Broome
Gary and Nancy DeJong
Steve and Mendi Everett
Michael and Cheryl Gayle
Becca Hafer
Beth Hafer
Shane and Lonna Jobson
Al and Paige Kemper
Keith and Michelle Lippy
Mark and Kimberly Luce
Aaragon and Malinda Markwell
Charles and Valerie Peterson
Mark and Alice Marie Peterson
Ross and Karen Riggs
Jeremy and Amy Sikes
David and Megan Southwell
Michael and Christine Speten
Jon and Kim Spink
John and Beverly Tolbert
Tom and Cheryl Welborn
Robert and Christy Westlake
Dave and Kathy Windham
Matthew and January Zimmerman

We deeply regret if any names have been omitted and request that this be brought to our attention.

Chronological Table of Events

The following table places some of the many remarkable incidents in the history of ABEO/ABWE within the context of a variety of parallel world events.

The ABEO/ABWE events appear in serif type directly after the year. World events follow in sans serif italic type.

1926

In June, Dr. Raphael C. Thomas resigns from the Foreign Missions Society.

B. F. Goodrich chemist Waldo Lonsbury Semon pioneers synthetic rubber.

1928

On December 17, the Incorporation Meeting of the Association of Baptists for Evangelism in the Orient is held. Lucy W. Peabody is elected chairman.

U.S. voters elect Herbert Hoover president with 444 electoral votes to the 87 received by his Democratic opponent Alfred E. Smith.

1930

ABEO missionaries in the first ABWE field, the Philippines:

Manila
R. C. and Norma Thomas
Paul and Margaret Culley
Bernice Hahn
Ellen Martien

Iloilo
Miss Alice Drake
Helen Hinkley
Bessie Traber
Edith Webster

Two new fields, Palawan and Cuyo, are offered to ABEO by a Presbyterian Mission. To minister to them effectively a boat is needed. Captain and Mrs. Ellis Skolfield offer themselves for missionary service in November, and a boat, the *Fukuin Maru* "Gospel Ship," is made available for sale to ABEO. On October 1, the first public meeting of the ABEO is held in Chelsea Baptist Church, Atlantic City, N.J.

On February 18, astronomers at the Lowell Observatory in Flagstaff, Ariz., discover Pluto and give the ninth planet its name.

A general world economic depression sets in.

Emigration from the United States for the first time in history exceeds immigration.

A civil disobedience campaign against the British in India begins in March. The All-India Trade Congress has empowered Mahatma Gandhi to begin the demonstrations.

1931

Rev. Jaffray gives a stirring appeal that the *Fukuin Maru* be used not only to reach the Philippines, but also the northern part of Borneo; thus claiming more of the "Orient" for Christ.

Columbia University physicist Harold C. Urey and two colleagues pioneer the production of atomic energy.

1932

An ex-leper, a convert won through the leprosarium work, is studying at Doane Evangelistic Institute.

The kidnapping of Charles A. Lindbergh, Jr., on March 1 makes world headlines.

1933

The treasurer, Miss Hudson, tells of several immediate needs: salaries; expenses for the Gospel Ship ($10 a day); passage for a new worker; rent for Manila Evangelistic Institute; $35 for scholarships for Bible school students; $50 annual assistance for evangelists in field work; and $20 a month in undesignated funds for the needs of the office.

The Nazis open the first German concentration camp at Dachau, near Munich. The facility is for Jews, Gypsies, and political prisoners.

1934

Ministries begin in the Sulu Archipelago, where 2,000,000 Moslems need to be reached; a Moro chief is led to the Lord on his deathbed, as three Moro priests listened to the explanation of Captain Skolfield and other missionaries.

A "Milk in Schools" scheme improves nutrition among British schoolchildren by supplying milk at little or no cost.

1935

Rev. Harold T. Commons, former vice president, becomes the president of the ABEO. Rev. Norman S. McPherson is the new vice president; and Rev. Howard Fulton is the new clerk. Mrs. Peabody remains on the board, and also continues her responsibilities as editor and publisher of the *Message*.

On November 15, President Roosevelt issues a proclamation terminating the present American government in the Philippines. Manuel Quezon was already elected the new president. Independence will be fully established in ten years.

1936

Luzon Baptist District Association opens in Manila area. Dr. Harold Commons returns from a five-month survey of the field.

39,000 U.S. maritime workers tie up all West Coast ports beginning in October in a strike that spreads to Eastern and Gulf Coast ports. The strike will last for nearly three months before seamen vote to accept tentative agreements.

1937

672 sign decisions for Christ in Opera House evangelistic meetings in Manila.

"I see one-third of a nation ill-housed, ill-clad, ill-nourished," reports President Roosevelt in his second inaugural address on January 20.

1938

ABEO expands for the first time to a land outside of the Philippines: the Island of Ceylon, in the capital city of Colombo.

Germany begins forced emigration of Jewish citizens.

1939

ABEO enters Peru and changes its name to the Association of Baptists for World Evangelism, Inc.; New Guinea is surveyed; Bukidnon, Mindanao, field is acquired.

Invasion of Poland by both the Germans and the Russians.

1940

James Ker, recently returned from Ceylon, is appointed deputation director.

On September 27, at Berlin, Germany, Italy, and Japan create a 10-year military and economic alliance called the Axis.

1941

Wm. Scherer meets and writes of the spiritual needs of the Ticuna Indians in Brazil and Colombia.

World War II explodes into a global conflict as German troops invade Soviet Russia and Japanese forces attack Pearl Harbor.

1942

ABWE enters Brazil and Colombia. Communications with missionaries and pastors are gradually cut off as the Japanese army advances through the Philippines.

Japanese forces take Manila on January 2, and invade the Dutch East Indies January 10. Japan suffers its first major sea loss in late January at the Battle of Macassar Strait, when U.S. and Dutch naval and air forces attack a Japanese convoy.

1943

In June, Harold Palmer, missionary pastor of First Baptist Church of Manila, dies as a result of complications from appendicitis while a prisoner of war in the Philippines. The Kohler family and Miss Lynip escape from the Philippines on a submarine.

For the first time, penicillin is applied to the treatment of chronic diseases.

Americans are told to "use it up, wear it out, make it do or do without." Shoes rationing begins in February. While the British are allowed only one pair per year, the U.S. ration is three pairs.

1944

The Victor Barnetts, veteran China missionaries who had escaped from the mainland in 1944, are appointed as ABWE missionaries to the Luichow Peninsula in South China. Donald Moffatt becomes deputation director.

On D-Day, June 6, 176,000 Allied troops land at Omaha Beach, Utah Beach, and other Normandy beaches under the supreme command of General Eisenhower.

1945

Liberation in the Philippines! Our missionaries are freed from various prison camps. "Mission House" in Germantown is given to ABWE; it will be used for many years for candidate classes.

World War II ends after nearly six years in which an estimated 54.8 million have died, most of them civilians. Millions more are left mutilated, homeless, orphaned, and impoverished.

1946

News begins to surface of a great harvest of souls in South Negros and Iloilo, as a result of the Filipinos faithfully continuing ministry during and after the war.

In Bombay, the social disabilities of the city's hanjans, or untouchables, are legally removed, but prejudice against them continues.

1947

National evangelists Nunez and Perez are joined by the Carders in opening Venezuela; Bible Institute buildings are under construction in Upper Amazon; Tibet and Dutch New Guinea are eyed for opening as ABWE fields.

Widespread food shortages continue in the wake of World War II and crop failures exacerbate the situation.

A Bedouin boy exploring a cave at Qumran, northwest of Palestine's Dead Sea, discovers an earthenware jar containing scrolls of parchment filled with all but two small parts of the Old Testament Book of Isaiah.

1948

Manila Evangelistic Institute becomes Manila Baptist Bible Seminary; Upper Amazon Bible Institute opens its doors; Jaymes Morgan is stoned in an open-air meeting in China.

The State of Israel is proclaimed May 14 as the British mandate over Palestine expires. Most of Britain's forces have withdrawn and most Arabs have fled the country.

1949

The first president of ABWE, Mrs. Peabody, dies on February 25.

Nineteen Eighty-Four by George Orwell is a frightening futuristic tale of a totalitarian state whose authorities exercise mind control. It is the origin of the phrase "Big Brother Is Watching You."

1950

Board structure of ABWE changes to Board and Advisory Council. The board consists of eight men and four women. The 4th Annual Meeting of the Evangelical Baptist Churches of the Jungle is held in Iquitos.

Communist North Korean forces invade the Republic of South Korea on June 25. So begins a three-year Korean War that will involve 16 nations against the communists.

1951

The "communization" of Tibet threatens to prevent the Millers from entering the field from India. ABWE enters Hong Kong.

Remington Rand introduces the Univac computer on a commercial basis for use by business firms and scientists.

1952

Donald MacKay begins his tenure in a full-time capacity with ABWE with a three-month trip to Asia. Four separate associations of indigenous churches totaling over 100 churches now exist in the Philippines. The board votes to open the fields of Japan and Chile.

Japanese tape-recorder maker Masaru Ibuka, who obtains a license from AT&T's Western Electric division, introduces the first pocket-size transistor radios under the name Sony.

1953

Protestant missionaries are ordered to leave the territories of Colombia in keeping with a new law prohibiting their ministries there; the church at Leticia is closed by order of the governor. Inaugural service is held in the small church at the "Port of Two Brothers."

A giant uranium deposit is found in Ontario's Algoma Basin. This discovery will make Canada a leading world supplier of the ore used to produce fuel for nuclear energy.

1954

Tent meetings in São Paulo have a "stormy" beginning. Mrs. Doane is with the Lord.

President Eisenhower modifies the U.S. pledge of allegiance in June, adding the phrase "under God."

1955

East Pakistan field is opened. Portable "tabernacles" are first used in Chile to replace tents. Indigenous "Baptist Workers Training School" is organized in Bukidnon.

On December 1, Rosa Parks, a seamstress in Montgomery, Ala., refuses to give up her seat on a downtown bus to a white man.

1956

A baby boy named "ABWE" is born in the Philippines.

With the claim that "History is on our side. We will bury you!" Nikita Khrushchev speaks to Western ambassadors at a Kremlin reception.

1957

Baptist Bible Seminary and Institute of São Paulo, Brazil, opens its doors. The *Gospel Launch* makes her maiden voyage in the Philippines.

A "Great Leap Forward" is launched by Mao Zedong in the People's Republic of China. More than half a billion peasants are put into 24,000 "people's communes." The people are guaranteed food, clothing, shelter, and childcare, but deprived of all private property.

1958

A portable tabernacle is erected in São Paulo, Brazil. First convert is baptized in East Pakistan. Baptist Church in Leticia, Colombia, is reopened by government order, but persecution continues. Outreach into Hebron, in East Pakistan, begins.

In October, Pan Am and BOAC inaugurate transatlantic jet service.

1959

Bahia, Brazil, becomes the site of new Central Brazil Field Council. First All-Amazon Conference is held in Iquitos. First challenge is given in the *Message* to pray for the evangelization of Quebec, Canada.

Cuban dictator Fulgencio Batista resigns January 1. Rebel leader Fidel Castro captures Santiago a day after taking the provincial capital of Santa Clara.

1960

ABWE begins its aviation church-planting ministry in Amazonas, Brazil, with one seaplane. Veteran missionaries Mr. and Mrs. Blakely Rogers are appointed as the first dorm parents for Oak Crest, the ABWE home for teenagers.

Brasília becomes Brazil's federal capital by order of President Kubitshek. The new city occupies a site that three years ago had only three non-Indian inhabitants.

1961

The first pastor is ordained from ABWE work in southern Brazil. First missionaries are appointed to serve under the Philippine Association of Baptists for World Evangelism. First graduation is held at Bethel Baptist Academy in Malaybalay, Philippines. Sunshine Baptist Clinic opens doors in Hong Kong.

The first manned space ship circles the earth on April 12 in 89.1 minutes at an altitude of 187.7 miles. Soviet astronaut Yuri Alekseyevich Gagarin makes the orbit in the space vehicle Vostok I.

1962

East Pakistan hospital site selection consultation is held. Leyte, Philippines, is surveyed. Central Brazil tent campaign meets with persecution. Bible Institute "Open House" is held in Santiago, Chile. The *Message* drops paid subscriptions. ABWE has 250 active missionaries. Maki San opens the first Christian book store in Kagoshima, Japan.

Washington and Moscow are joined in a tense nuclear confrontation in October, in what becomes known as the Cuban missile crisis.

1963

New hymnals are published by the ABWE press in the Philippines. Ministry in Hilongos, Leyte, begins. Six portable tabernacles have been put into use for starting new churches in São Paulo, Brazil, since 1954.

Snakebite and salvation are experienced at Jisoike camp in Japan. The *Island Reaper* joins the *Gospel Launch* in Philippine evangelism.

President Kennedy is assassinated.

Dr. De Bakey uses an artificial heart for the first time.

Supreme Court rules that reading the Lord's Prayer or verses from the Bible in schools is unconstitutional.

1964

The Pakistan government grants a long-awaited short-wave radio license and duty-free import permits for hospital equipment to ABWE. Construction begins at the hospital site. Tent campaigns result in new churches in the Philippines, and a new student center is opened in North Luzon.

Zambia is created October 24 out of Northern Rhodesia and Barotseland.

President Johnson announces a vast increase in U.S. aid to South Vietnam in December.

1965

A nine-day Islamic Conference is held in Chittagong, East Pakistan. Japan missionaries Paul and Vada Shook become house parents at Oak Crest. Christian book store opens in Recife, Brazil. Missionaries safe as war breaks out between East Pakistan and India.

U.S. planes bomb North Vietnam on March 2. 3,500 U.S. Marines land at Da Nang on March 8–9 in the first deployment of U.S. combat troops in Vietnam.

Pakistan and much of India suffer widespread starvation as monsoon rains fail and crops are destroyed in a withering drought.

1966

Hilongos Christian Center is opened in Leyte, Philippines. In March, Memorial Christian Hospital in Malumghat is opened for patients.

The Tennessee Valley Authority (TVA) orders construction of a one-million-kilowatt nuclear power plant at Decatur, Ala.

1967

ABWE finally formally enters New Guinea. A 40/40 plan is instituted in celebration of ABWE's 40th year.

The Six-Day Arab-Israeli War begins June 5, following months of conflict between Israel and Syria.

1968

ABWE enters the country of Spain. The ABWE—Canada Executive Committee is formed. A permanent downtown home for Baptist Bible Seminary and Institute of São Paulo, Brazil, is provided.

Martin Luther King, Jr., is shot dead April 4 as he steps out on the balcony of his Memphis motel room.

Senator Robert Kennedy is assassinated in June after victory in the presidential primary.

1969

On June 9, Hong Kong Baptist Bible Institute holds Commencement service for its first three graduates. ABWE holds its candidate classes at Baptist Bible College, Clarks Summit, Pa., for

the first time. 25,000 Filipino boys and girls use the VBS materials produced by ABWE's literature department this year.

Man walks on the moon for the first time on July 21.

Washington announces on December 19 that it will relax restrictions on U.S. trade with Beijing.

1970

Australia is opened as a new ABWE field.

Some 152,000 U.S. postal workers strike 671 locations in March. The Army is sent in to sort the mail and, in August, the Post Office Department becomes the U.S. Postal Service.

1971

In June, as Dr. Harold T. Commons steps down after 36 years, Rev. Wendell W. Kempton becomes president. In July, the home office is relocated to Cherry Hill, N.J.

The Republic of Zaire is created on October 27. President Mobutu Sese Seko (formerly Joseph D. Mobutu) renames the Democratic Republic of Congo. Even the Congo River is renamed the Zaire.

1972

The Cedarville College basketball team visits the Far East. B. Donald Sutherland becomes ABWE treasurer.

Bangladesh (formerly East Pakistan) proclaims itself a sovereign state, with Sheik Mujibur Rahman as prime minister.

1973

Paraguay and Togo are opened as new ABWE fields. In September, the first Missionary Enrichment Conference is held at Emmanuel Baptist Church in Toledo, Ohio.

A ceasefire in Vietnam on January 28 ends direct involvement of U.S. ground troops in the Southeast Asian conflict. America's combat death toll has reached 45,958. The last U.S. troops leave South Vietnam on March 29.

1974

Leyte Baptist Clinic is built. Literature division building is supplied by God in Chittagong, Bangladesh. ABWE enters Paraguay. Ministry to the blind people of Togo, West Africa, begins.

President Nixon resigns in disgrace on August 9—the first U.S. president ever to quit office. President Gerald R. Ford is sworn in on August 9.

Japan's Prime Minister Kakuei Tanaka resigns November 26 in the face of financial scandals.

1975

Gene Gurganus' new water pump is demonstrated in Bangladesh. A Christian book booth is set up at the National Book Exhibition in Chittagong.

Cambodia's new Khmer Rouge government begins a wholesale slaughter of intellectuals, political enemies, dissidents, and peasants.

1976

Project Heartbeat for Bangladesh seeks to raise $400,000 for medical and spiritual needs. Construction begins on ABWE Camp in Okuchi, Japan. Paraguay and USA are new ABWE fields.

Apple Computer is founded in a California garage to produce personal computers.

In September, Swedish voters end 44 years of socialist rule.

1977

The Gospel of John, a Bible story book, and a pamphlet about the Lord Jesus are ready for publication in Muslim Bengali. The Bengali Common Language New Testament is completed. Shawnee Baptist Church, the first begun under ABWE USA, is born in New Jersey.

The first MRI (Magnetic Resonance Imaging) scanner is tested July 2 by Brooklyn, N.Y., medical researcher Raymond V. Damadian. His diagnostic tool will be used to detect cancer and other soft-tissue abnormalities without exposing patients to the radiation of X-rays.

1978

Executive Board approves entering Portugal for church planting. Bible training school for the hearing impaired is opened in Kagoshima, Japan. ABWE decides to enter Norway.

Washington recognizes the People's Republic of China in December, announcing that it will sever diplomatic ties with longtime ally Taiwan as of January 1, 1979.

1979

Through an estate planning arrangement, a Delta Airlines captain becomes the intermediate source of the ABWE airfield in Concord, Georgia. ABWE enters The Gambia.

Panama takes over operation of the Panama Canal on October 1 under terms of a 1978 treaty establishing a 20-year transition from U.S. control.

1980

Mrs. Corinth Commons (wife of Dr. Harold Commons), Chuck Cook, Bernice Hahn, Michael and Gladys Martin, and Mrs. Karolyn Kempton (wife of Dr. Wendell Kempton) are all taken to heaven. South Africa is a new ABWE field. Seminary ministry begins in Kagoshima, Japan.

Liberia President William R. Tolbert, Jr., is ousted in a military coup and is executed along with 27 other high officials. A People's Redemptive Council suspends the Constitution on April 25 and assumes all executive power, with General (formerly Master Sergeant) Samuel K. Doe as president.

1981

Change in the Home Office administration is begun by Dr. Kempton. Experienced missionaries are to be appointed as regional administrators. First AWANA club meetings in the Philippines are held. The Church Ministries Institute is opened in South Africa.

Britain's Prince Charles marries Lady Diana Spencer at St. Paul's Cathedral, London, in July.

1982

The Karolyn Kempton Memorial Christian Hospital in Togo, and the Aklan Hospital in Panay, Philippines, are built. For the former, $415,000 of gifts were matched by an anonymous donor. ABWE USA director Floyd Davis dies of cancer. Interface 1982 brings missions educators and ABWE personnel together.

In January, a Boeing 737 crashes into Washington's 14th Street bridge after takeoff from National Airport; only five of the 79 aboard are rescued and four others are killed on the bridge.

1983

Kenya becomes an ABWE field. The Fellowship of ABWE Churches in Hong Kong is dedicated. The Cuyonon New Testament is launched in Palawan. "Southern Cone of South America Conference" is held in Argentina.

Lebanese terrorists blow up the U.S. Embassy at Beirut on April 18, killing 63 people. Two U.S. marines are killed and 13 wounded August 29 when mortar shells and rockets land in an airport compound during battles between Lebanese Army and Shiite Muslim and Druse forces.

1984

The ABWE board names England and France as new fields. The ENCORE Program is initiated to inform volunteers of opportunities for ministry on the various fields.

President Reagan is reelected with 525 electoral votes to 13 for former vice president Walter Mondale.

1985

The Karolyn Kempton Hospital is dedicated in June. In September, the Amazon Baptist Hospital is dedicated. The Carol Roduner memorial chapel enters its first full year of use near Iquitos, Peru.

A Mexico City area earthquake on September 19, measuring 7.8 on the Richter scale, kills more than 5,000.

1986

Drs. Kempton and Ebersole quietly minister to Baptist churches in communist Romania. Pastor Will Davis becomes new ABWE vice president. Asia Baptist Theological Seminary is inaugurated in April.

On January 28, all seven astronauts aboard the U.S. space shuttle Challenger *die as their craft explodes 73 seconds after liftoff from Cape Canaveral.*

1987

The first building team goes to The Gambia to begin building the medical clinic. The Po Lam Baptist Elderly Center is opened in Hong Kong.

Gene-altered bacteria to aid agriculture are tested in April despite warnings of possible long-term danger.

1988

The board votes to open Italy as an ABWE field. Canada is also recognized as a new ABWE field. ABWE's first ministry team to Central and Eastern Europe begins to minister quietly in Eastern Europe, and Hungary and Romania are targeted for church planting.

Moscow agrees April 14 to withdraw Soviet forces from Afghanistan (the first group leaves May 17), promises to have all 115,000 out by mid-February 1989, and agrees to restore a nonaligned Afghan state.

1989

Mexico City becomes a new ABWE target for ministry. West Germany is also approved as an ABWE field. On March 6, dedication of the Ndungu Kebbeh Medical and Literacy Centers is held. ABWE's Christmas Project sends Bibles to Russia.

Soviet citizens gain rights and other Eastern Europeans overthrow despots in spontaneous uprisings after Beijing cracks down on dissidents with a bloody massacre.

1990

Project HOPE (Helping Open People's Eyes) takes the gospel to thousands in the Philippines. "Thrust 1990" is used of God to bring a harvest of new missionaries.

Germany reunites and the U.S.S.R. crumbles as Iraqi aggression threatens to ignite a Mideast conflagration.

1991

Twelve churches have graduated from ABWE USA. Ukraine is to become the next Central and Eastern Europe field.

Operation Desert Storm begins February 24 and ends in 100 hours with Iraqi forces defeated. President Bush has spurned the advice of General Colin Powell, chairman of the Joint Chiefs of Staff, to give economic sanctions more time to work.

1992

In April, the ABWE board approves entry into Ghana, West Africa. In November, Singapore is opened as a specialized field, with emphasis on theological education. Ground breaking is held for new ABWE headquarters in Harrisburg, Pa.

U.S. voters elect Arkansas governor William Jefferson Blythe "Bill" Clinton to the presidency, rejecting George Bush's reelection bid as economic recession shows few signs of abating.

1993

Romania is opened as the newest ABWE Central and Eastern European country. The "Miracle on the Hill" is dedicated. Central America becomes the newest ABWE region.

AT&T announces August 16 that it will pay $12.6 billion to acquire McCaw Cellular Communications, the nation's largest cellular telephone company.

1994

George Collins is appointed to direct Global Access Partnerships (GAP), a new ministry partnering with national leaders and churches.

President Clinton announces May 26 that he is renewing China's most-favored-nation status despite continuing human rights violations, saying that MFN status will no longer be linked to human rights.

1995

The Resource and Training Center is dedicated in Odessa, Ukraine. Slovakia is a new ABWE field. Dr. Russ Ebersole, Jr., is appointed vice president for missionary ministries. The Standard Bengali Common Language Bible translation is completed.

Aum Shinri Kyo cult attacks commuters on Tokyo subway with sarin gas.

O.J. Simpson trial attracts nationwide attention.

1996

On January 14, the William Carey Academy opens in Chittagong, Bangladesh. Cambodia is approved as a new ABWE field, as are Bosnia and Uruguay. Construction begins on the Lisbon Training Center in Portugal.

Taliban leaders seize Afghan capital of Kabul.

"Dolly" the sheep is cloned from adult cells.

1997

The Harold T. Commons Administrative Center and the Edward C. Bomm Financial Center are dedicated at the Home Office. In June, Mr. Bomm, who attended the dedication, is with the Lord. Mongolia becomes the newest ABWE field.

Hong Kong returns to Chinese rule.

The Nobel Prize in Medicine goes to Stanley B. Prusiner (U.S.) for discovery of prions.

1998

Project HOPE II, is held in the Philippines. The ABWE board appoints 68 candidates for career missions.

Europeans agree on a single currency: the euro.

President Clinton is impeached along party lines in the House of Representatives.

1999

Thailand, first served by Filipino missionaries with PABWE, is opened as a career field. Vietnam, Nepal, Costa Rica, and Cuba are also approved as ABWE fields. Ground breaking is held for the International Training Center building.

War erupts in Kosovo.

A magnitude 7.4 earthquake in Turkey kills more than 15,600 and leaves 600,000 homeless.

2000

An ABWE Gala Celebration of the Greatness of God is held. The Muslim Bible translation is completed. The West African countries of Benin and Liberia are approved as ABWE fields.

Widely feared effects of the "Millennium Bug" and other phenomena prove to be unfounded as the year 2000 dawns.

2001

In February, the first Global Consultation is held, with leaders from all fields present. In March, Dr. Wendell Kempton steps down and Dr. Michael Loftis is installed as the new ABWE president. In April, an ABWE plane is shot down in Peru, killing Roni and Charity Bowers. The International Training Center is dedicated. New ABWE fields opened in 2001 are Russia, Malaysia, Croatia, Trinidad & Tobago, Nicaragua, and the Republic of Ireland. Mexico was transferred from ABWE North America to Central America region. Dr. William Commons is appointed vice president in charge of strategic initiatives and research.

Terrorists attack the World Trade Center and the Pentagon using three U.S. commercial airliners.

Passengers of a fourth plane fight with the terrorists and the plane crashes in a Pennsylvania field.